The day the pitcher ran late . . .

"What about that guy who got lost going to an Atlanta Braves game?" a friend asked when I told him I was looking for famous lost people. "What guy?" My friend couldn't remember.

I called the P.R. man for the Atlanta Braves. "Oh yeah," said Glen Ferra. "Pasqual Perez. The story's all true. He'd just gotten his driver's license I think. I don't even know how much English he spoke. He got on the highway that goes around the perimeter of the city. He went around the 38-mile perimeter three times looking for the stadium. Then he ran out of gas. I don't remember how he finally got there—a cab, hitchhiked—but he was too late to pitch."

I'll Never Get Lost Again

The Complete Guide to Improving Your Sense of Direction

Linda Zitomer Grekin

RDR Books
Oakland, California

I'll Never Get Lost Again:
The Complete Guide to Improving Your Sense of Direction

RDR Books
4456 Piedmont Avenue
Oakland, California 94611

ISBN 1-57143-069-5
Library of Congress Catalog Card Number: 98-067941

Cover design by Jennifer Braham
Book design by Paula Morrison
Edited by Bob Drews
Title consultant: Peter Beren

Distributed in Canada by General Distribution Services, 325
Humber College Boulevard, Toronto, Ontario M9W7C3

Distributed in England and Europe by Airlift Book Company,
8 The Arena, Mollison Avenue, Enfield, Middlesex EN3 7NJ
England

Distributed in Australia and New Zealand by Astam Books pty Ltd
57–61 John Street Leichardt, New South Wales 2038, Australia

Printed in the United States of America by Thomson-Shore

This book is dedicated to my husband Roger, without whom I would be lost, and to my children, Joe, Josh, and Emily, whose practical advice and delightful sense of humor have guided and supported me for years.

I extend special thanks to Dr. Stephen Kaplan, Professor of Psychology at the University of Michigan, who helped me focus my search for information, provided me with resources, and took the time to explain things I didn't understand. I also thank all those people who put aside embarrassment to share their "getting lost stories" with me.

Contents

Lost and Found

I knew they would laugh. They stood behind me, my husband and sons, as I looked out into the hall. There was no one there. It was quiet and there was nothing to be seen but a long stretch of carpet reaching down the corridor. I searched for a clue. I listened for a sound that would help me. Finally I just gave up and walked out, turning right as I exited the room. The laughter burst out behind me. I tried to be good humored. Of course I'd turned the wrong way out of this hotel room. I turn the wrong way out of every hotel room. As usual, I didn't have a clue as to which way to go. I was lost, again.

Millions of competent people living meaningful, productive lives become easily disoriented and are often unable to find their way. Are you one of them, stuck in airports and parking lots, in shopping centers and office buildings, unable to find your way out of the emotional cul-de-sac that is navigational incompetence? I know I am, and I have lots of company: men and women, old and young, doctors and teachers, housewives and computer experts. People often look at us and shake their heads, disbelieving. Sometimes they laugh. Sometimes they talk to us in a slow, patronizing tone as if it would take a great deal of patience and a long time to make us understand. They don't realize that we have a real disability. We are directionally challenged.

I have been lost all over the world. I have been lost in small villages and big cities. I've been lost on fast-moving expressways and meandering country roads. When I was young, it never occurred to me that there were people who saw the world as a map, navigated cities without trouble, knew which way to turn when they walked out of a hotel room. But as I grew older I realized there were people who had something that was not my birthright—a sense of direction. They were advantaged in a way I could never dream of. It was like growing up poor and suddenly discovering that others had money, lots of it, and could afford things beyond my reach. I tried to accept my fate. I'd make fun of the fact that I had no sense of direction, but deep down I was disturbed. I couldn't explain why I was unable to find my way. Why could some people glance at a map and quickly find a restaurant, a hotel, or a grocery store in a strange town? How could people slide easily onto a freeway, certain they were headed toward Toledo instead of Escanaba? How did they know, and why didn't I?

It's a maze out there for me. I look at a map, but the paper markings don't tell me where I am. There seems to be no connection in my brain between those strange lines cartographers label roads and what I see. The simplest wayfinding tasks disorient me. My husband and children laugh at me because I never know where the elevator is when I leave a hotel room. I can figure out how to get to my husband's office only if I always enter the building the same way. I would never attempt to go somewhere new without intense preparation. When I have to go somewhere important, my husband takes me there the night before. He writes out directions, highlights maps, and draws me pictures. These dress rehearsals work, but they are frustrating and often make me feel stupid and dependent. Why can't I easily drive to another city without my husband's help in advance? Why do I need carefully written directions? Why can't I take advantage of shortcuts like everyone else? What's the matter with me?

People can hear and smell and see. They touch and taste. They have five senses. These five senses make the world come alive. They can look at a flower and see how delicate it is, but when they touch its velvet softness, when they smell that fleeting wisp of wild sweetness, its delicacy and beauty are made more real.

Some people also refer to a sixth sense, an intuitive feeling that often influences a person's actions. You might hear someone say, "I don't want to enter that room. I just have a feeling that something bad is going to happen."

Not much has been said, however, about the seventh sense—the sense of direction. It allows people to picture where they are in relation to things around them and enables them, no matter where they are or how they are turned, to say, "That's north!" How can people do that? I want to walk down a street in a strange city and say nonchalantly to the person next to me, "By the way, that's north."

For years people made fun of me. They told me that if I paid attention I could find my way. They were wrong. I pay attention, but I can't find my way. Why?

The Directionally Challenged—
Who Are They?

When I started writing this book, I wasn't sure how many people were directionally challenged. Every once in a while you read a newspaper article like the one printed in the *Detroit Free Press* on March 24, 1998 headlined, "Tapes suggest inept, threatening mobsters." Two alleged Mafia members shot out the windows of a Detroit business, but couldn't find the expressway to make their getaway. Or there will be a letter to Ann Landers from a distraught person who always gets lost and is questioning her sanity. There's even a book titled *Explorers Who Got Lost*. But for the most part, people don't talk about this disability, and I hadn't heard of any scientific studies on the subject. I knew there had to be people besides my mother, myself, and my daughter who routinely got lost; I wondered where I could find them. I wanted to know that I was not alone, that there were other normal, intelligent, successful people out there for whom north and south meant nothing, adults who courageously walked strange streets and pretended that maps made sense. How could I find them?

As it turned out, writing a book on this subject was a little like doing one about sex. The problem isn't getting people to start talking, it's getting them to stop. All I had to do was begin a conversation with, "I'm writing a book about people with no sense of direction," and people would instantly cut me off to say things like:

"I'm always lost." or

"I always turn the wrong way when I step out of an elevator." or

"I can't find my way anywhere." or

"My wife says I couldn't find my way out of a cardboard box."

It made me wonder just what percentage of the population was directionally disabled or, as a friend pointedly corrected me, directionally challenged.

Many people who think they have a good sense of direction actually don't. Just because someone can follow directions doesn't mean he or she has a good sense of direction. If the directions are clear, I can follow them.

Some claim they have a good sense of direction because they know how to use a map. Map reading is a learned skill. It is not the same as intuitively finding your way.

How do you know if you have a good sense of direction? Expressway behavior is a good test. People with a good sense of direction do not panic when they are driving on an expressway and are forced to exit due to an accident. They do not dissolve into tears or call 911 on their car phone. They just pick another road that goes in the "right" direction. It's no problem for them to loop or twist or cut across back roads. They always know where they are. To use the old expression, they "follow their nose."

People with an OK sense of direction, when forced off an expressway, can follow side roads fairly easily as long as those roads don't twist too much or wind too far afield. They have a general sense of where they are going and can maintain their emotional stability while they find their way.

People with no sense of direction don't have to worry about detouring off expressways because, unless forced to do so, we don't get on them. If, God forbid, we do find ourselves in those circumstances, we will decompensate. If you ever see a woman standing on the side of the road, hysterical, stop. It's me.

Trying to get a handle on just how many among us are directionally challenged was not easy. We live in a world of experts who have answers to questions we haven't even thought of, and consultants who will borrow your watch to tell you what time it is. I am a school librarian, used to looking for obscure facts, finding answers to strange questions and now, thanks to the Internet, having a planet full of research at my fingertips. Yet I couldn't find one expert, consultant, or body of research on this subject.

I called psychologists in Michigan and Wisconsin and found that there is a lot of research on spatial abilities—the ability to remember what you see, the ability to transfer a map route to your brain, the ability to rotate figures in your mind—but I couldn't find anyone who had applied that research to people lacking a sense of direction. I decided to do my own research.

With the help of a psychologist at the University of Michigan I designed a survey to identify the directionally challenged person and set out to find people willing to talk.

It was 16 degrees and windy when I staked out my position in front of a neighborhood grocery in Ann Arbor, Michigan. Obviously no one was anxious to stand outside and chat. But 20 people were intrigued enough by my questions about directional sense that they agreed to fill out the survey. Eleven of them, six women and five men, claimed to have no sense of direction at all.

I called a friend who teaches English at the University of Michigan and who can find his way anywhere. He agreed to supplement my efforts. A few days later he called with very interesting results. Of the 100 students in his lecture classes, 20 claimed to have no sense of direction. I talked to others— friends, colleagues, strangers, people on the Internet—and got findings like these:

⇨ At a dinner party, four of the six people I was seated with were directionally challenged.

⇨ At a going-away party for a colleague in my husband's medical division, 10 of the 34 people said they had no sense of direction.

⇨ My husband asked if any of the 90 students in his second-year medical school class had no sense of direction. Nine students raised their hands.

⇨ I attended a small seminar. Three of the six people on hand were directionally challenged.

⇒ Of the 12 people in my bridge group, five have no sense of direction.

⇒ I surveyed the teachers at my school. Of 51 who responded, 26 were challenged.

⇒ The son of a friend surveyed 10 of his Internet friends. Five claimed to have no sense of direction.

Looking over the results of my surveys, I realized that I had sampled a wide variety of people—college students, teachers and school administrators, medical students, friends, strangers who shop at the same grocery store, people responding over the Internet. My sample was diverse, though not what a professional statistician would call a true random sample. Does that make a difference? Not to me. Ten percent to 20 percent of the people sampled had no sense of direction, suggesting to me that an equal percentage of the population of the United States, or at least 25–50 million Americans, are directionally challenged.

Only Six Senses

My survey results and many personal interviews confirmed that operating without a seventh sense is difficult, confusing and frustrating.

"My husband has a terrible sense of direction," said a no-nonsense college professor. "Several years ago we moved to a new subdivision. The first two nights my husband drove home from work he had to stop and call me because he couldn't find our new house. Finally he learned one way to get from our house to work and back. He never varies his route. He's afraid that if he does he'll get lost."

"They need to pin a name tag on me," said a warm, funny teacher. "Every year we take the kindergartners to the zoo. I dread it. I can't find my way out of that place. The kids all know. They say, 'Just stay here, Mrs. Muller. We'll come back for you.' I'm terrible," she continued. "One day I was trying to find Hudson's Department Store. I got confused and had no idea which way to go. Then a Hudson's delivery truck passed me. Yes! I just followed the truck to the store."

Following someone isn't always the answer.

"I used to be an ambulance driver in Los Angeles," a young woman related. "I had a map and everything seemed to be fine. One day I got called to an accident and couldn't find this place. I was panicking when a fire truck sped past me. With a sigh of relief I followed it. I ended up at an accident, but it was the wrong one. Now I work in a research lab."

My mother tells of attending a funeral near her home. My dad couldn't go, but because the funeral parlor was almost right around the corner she went herself. She had no trouble finding the place and after the service got in line to drive to the cemetery. She was last in the long line of black flagged cars slowly proceeding through traffic. But last one in, first one out. Following the cemetery service my mother got in her car and began winding through the cemetery passing old friends and relatives buried here and there among the tall trees and quiet pools. Suddenly she glanced in her rear view mirror and realized that a huge line of cars was following her expecting that she would lead them out of the cemetery. She had no idea how to get out, but figured that if she kept driving she'd eventually come to an exit. She kept driving. So did the 30 cars following her. She began to panic. Finally the driver behind her became so irritated that he sped across the grass and passed her, leading the group from death back to life.

Doctors' offices with several corridors and multiple examining rooms can be especially hazardous. "It's so humiliating," said a short, blond woman. "You're all done and the nurse tells you to get dressed and check out. I get dressed just fine, but when I go out the exam room door I don't have any idea which way to turn to get out. You feel like an idiot standing there peering down the hall."

Doctors' offices are one thing, shopping is another. "I was worried when I became the mother of a daughter," explained Janice, a lovely, intense young woman, "because I can't go to malls. I get lost. How could I go clothes shopping with my daughter? As it happens I didn't have to worry. My daughter has a great sense of direction and she leads me around."

Janice could take advice from my friend Rita, a born shopper. The fact that she has no sense of direction doesn't keep her from any store, big or small, free standing or in a mall. "I love to go to Marshall Fields in Chicago," she told me. "When I'm done shopping I put my packages down, open my purse and take out my compass. I follow it north through the store and out on to North Michigan Avenue where I want to be. You'd be surprised," she told me, "how many people see me in the store following a compass and ask me for directions."

A compass only works sometimes. "I thought it would be good to have a compass in the car," said a man I had known for years. "I got one of those compasses you stick on the dashboard. I fastened it, but then I had to make some adjustments to make it more accurate. I used a magnetic screwdriver. From that time on the compass always pointed to the screw. It didn't prove very helpful."

Many people who are directionally challenged don't advertise it. Take my neighbor, Dave "Wrong Way" Wiss. "I've been known to be on the right street going the wrong way for five or 10 miles before I realize it," he told me. "I always turn the wrong way." Dave is a tall, athletic dentist who always seems confident and in control. He runs and skis. He's biked all over the country. He rode across Michigan, pedaled through the hills and valleys of Pennsylvania, and braved the cold lonely roads near the Canadian Rockies. Dave is often lost, yet only his good friends know this. The directionally challenged are indistinguishable from the "normals." Take Greg, a 36-year-old computer analyst. His office is in a large building with a lot of twists and turns. Everything is painted white and there are no landmarks along the corridors and hallways. Not even a picture breaks the long white expanse of wall after wall after wall. "When I first started working here," he admitted, "I couldn't find my office. I got lost every day. It took me a month to walk in the front door and, without making a wrong turn, go directly to my room." Did anyone know? Of course not. He walked down one white corridor after another, head up, chin out, as if he knew where he was going.

A slim banker with a wonderful, dry sense of humor surprised me one day by saying, "I can't drive through that neighborhood. Once I turn in I'm never sure how to get out." The neighborhood is lovely, with big trees, rolling hills and winding streets. "I don't even try to go through those neighborhoods where the streets aren't straight east/west, north/south," he said.

My daughter, Emily, entered junior high school in the seventh grade. Although the building was larger than her elementary school and the classes were more demanding, she seemed to enjoy it. She attended every day and never balked at going. One morning, a few months into the first semester, she came downstairs and announced that she wasn't going to school. "Are you sick?" I asked, touching her forehead.

"No. I just can't go."

"Was someone mean to you? Did something happen I need to know about?"

"No, Margaret's sick. "

"Why can't you go to school when she's sick?"

"Margaret's in all of my classes. I follow her. If she isn't there I don't know where to go."

Everybody admits that getting lost is no fun. "I don't travel much," one man confessed. "Trips are a major thing. They require so much preparation to assure I won't get lost that it's easier to stay home. Why go somewhere when it makes you so anxious?"

"There are a lot of places I just don't go to because I won't drive on the expressway," one woman told me. "I'm afraid I won't know where to get off, and if I exit in the wrong place, I won't know how to get on again."

"I don't go anywhere new by myself," another woman admitted. "There's no place I want to go that badly. Either someone takes me, or I stay home."

It's frightening when you don't know where you are. Nancy, an obstetrical nurse, is the calm, reassuring professional who can make patients get beyond fear. She reasons with them and finds ways to make sure they don't panic. But take her out of the maternity ward, put her on a plane to the Caribbean and she's in trouble. After spending the morning sightseeing on one trip, she headed back to her hotel to meet her husband for lunch. "I thought I knew the way, but when I started walking, I realized that I didn't know where I was. I decided it would be easy to find my way if I could see the water. I kept walking down street after street, but they all looked the same.

Every hut I passed looked like the one before and the next one. I tried to ask some schoolchildren for directions, but they didn't understand English. I totally panicked. I was in tears." Finally Nancy spotted the water, and was able to make her way back to the hotel.

A psychiatrist, who makes her living solving other people's problems, told me about getting lost while attending a meeting in Tokyo. She had to walk from her hotel to a conference center several blocks away. This was easy. She memorized her route before she set out. One block, then turn left. Two blocks, then turn right. She arrived with no trouble, but when she tried to return to her hotel the doctor's memory failed her and she got turned around. She was unable to read the street signs, and the buildings were not numbered consecutively, since in Japan buildings are often numbered for the year in which they were built. She wandered in circles getting increasingly agitated. Finally the psychiatrist spotted her salvation—a police kiosk. She repeated the name of her hotel several times in English. The policemen nodded in a friendly way and returned to work. Back outside, frightened and disoriented, she did what any sensible person lacking the seventh sense would do. She began to cry. "I pictured myself wandering the streets of Tokyo forever," she said. "I thought I'd never get back to the United States." Finally, in desperation, she hailed a cab. After repeating the name of her hotel several times and getting no response, she indicated with circling hands that she wanted the cab driver to circle the streets. He did. Eventually she spotted her hotel.

A physician, nationally known for his research in hypertension, offered a similar story. He flew into a major American city to attend a conference. He rented a car and drove to his hotel. Determined to save money, he avoided the hotel lot and parked on the street. He checked in, washed up, and headed out for dinner. Then he made the classic mistake. He went out of the hotel a different way than he had come in. "I couldn't find my car. It was dark and I obviously wasn't in a very good neighborhood. I remember spending an hour looking for my car in ever widening circles. As I turned down one street after another I thought to myself, 'I could get killed here.'"

The person with no sense of direction can get lost anywhere. "I'm like Hansel and Gretel," said a kindergarten teacher. "I have to drop bread crumbs to find my way back. If the birds eat them, I'm done for."

"I took care of my granddaughter for the day," related a smart fifth-grade teacher. "When it was time to take her home, we got in the car and I pulled out the directions to my son's house. My granddaughter stared at me. 'Don't you know where I live Grandma?' she asked."

"I still get lost in the medical center," admitted a young, engaging physician. "There is a certain way I go from my office to my lab. I can't go any other way. I turn left at this blackboard with a lost glove pinned on it. If someone claims the glove I'm finished."

A woman very involved in her community explained, "Even in town I have to plot out a route, and sometimes I go a longer way to avoid getting lost."

"Just because I got someplace," a 30-something computer specialist stated, "doesn't mean I can get back."

Incompetence and Implications

People have different abilities. Some are good at math, while others must use their fingers to add, walk the other way when people start listing percentages, or have nightmares figuring out tax returns and balancing checkbooks.

Some people are mechanical. They can fix anything, while others consult phone books, comb through ads, and beg friends for the number of a reliable handyman.

So then why write a book about people who have no sense of direction? Isn't that just another difference among people? Why not write a book about people who hate math, or people who aren't mechanical?

Of course I started to write about people with no sense of direction because I am one of those people, and I always wanted to know why. But not having a sense of direction, I found out, means more than just having trouble finding your way. This lack of a directional sense can play a part in the development of self-esteem and self-confidence. It determines in many ways how people will live their lives and what kind of a personality they will have.

People who aren't good at math or can't put things together are accepted. Saying "I'm not a math person" is not embarrassing. There is no stigma attached to a lack of mechanical ability. People with no sense of direction, however, often find themselves in situations that make them feel stupid, ashamed, and incompetent. A friend of mine, for example, told me that one night she got a call at 9 p.m. from her husband, who'd been out of town. He told her that he'd lost his car keys and asked her to come to the airport with another set. "I was hysterical," she said. "I knew I could never drive to the airport by myself. I'd get lost. My husband must have been temporarily insane or extremely desperate to ask me to do that. I called a friend who came right over, but she misunderstood the situation. She expected to stay with my kids while I went to the airport. I had to admit to her that I couldn't get to the airport alone. It was so humiliating. My friend had to deliver the keys to my husband while I sat at home, mortified."

A very competent woman who has traveled throughout the United States and Europe admitted that she, too, has no sense of direction. She told me about an experience in Copenhagen, Denmark, where she and her friends decided to go shopping separately and arranged to meet in the central square later in the day. She went into a store that had just the kind of clothes she liked, tried on a few, and mentioned to the saleswoman that the store had really nice things. She spent a delightful afternoon going in and out of this and other shops. Just before it was time to meet her friends, she found herself in a lovely store. She bought a scarf and told the saleswomen how much she liked the merchandise. "That's what you said when you were here two hours ago," the saleswoman replied. The woman had been walking in circles all afternoon.

People with no sense of direction are often forced into embarrassing situations. Have you ever seen one of those movies in which an airplane pilot suffers a heart attack and one of the passengers has to take over the controls? The passenger knows nothing about airplanes, but the control tower "talks him in." I had a similar experience. Actually I wasn't in an airplane, and no one had a heart attack. But the "talk in" part was the same.

I had a doctor's appointment at a community hospital I had never been to before. I arrived with time to spare carrying detailed directions to the doctor's office. Turning into the long driveway, I was surprised to see that there were separate buildings set in the woods. The road curved and turned until I lost track of where I had entered. I passed Back Pain, Head Trauma, Nursing Home, Emergency but didn't see Dermatology, the building I needed. I drove around, went through the yellow parking lot, red parking lot, blue parking lot, green parking lot. When I again passed Back Pain, Head Trauma, Nursing Home, and Emergency, I began to panic. I pulled to a stop in front of Emergency and told myself that I was too old to be humiliated. I picked up my car phone and dialed the dermatology clinic, told them I had been driving down driveways and past buildings for what seemed like forever and couldn't find them.

They "talked me in." The receptionist told me not to worry and to keep the phone at my ear. In a slow, reassuring voice she directed me past Emergency, through the green lot, around Back Pain and Head Trauma and Nursing Home, to the Dermatology building. I walked in, trying to ignore the knowing smiles around me, wishing I was invisible.

This feeling of humiliation is not uncommon among the directionally challenged.

"I went to visit my family in Massachusetts," a woman told me. "I had my two daughters with me. One day I took the two girls to visit a friend in New Hampshire. Somehow I ended up in Maine. I had to call and tell my friend I was in the wrong state. I was mortified. I still don't understand what happened."

"I went to Paris after my graduation from college. Naturally I wanted to see everything. I took the *Métro* to the Eiffel Tower. I walked out of the station and looked around. I didn't see the Tower. I thought I had gone to the right place, but the Eiffel Tower was nowhere in sight. I was so used to getting lost that I knew what to do. I stopped a policeman and asked where I could find the Eiffel Tower. *'Mademoiselle,'* he said, 'Look up!'"

People with no sense of direction have heard others tell them so many times, "If you'd just pay attention you could find your way," that they feel stupid. They know they are paying attention, yet they inevitably get lost. It follows that something must be terribly wrong with them. "I thought I had some kind of brain damage, that I was born with something wrong," a quiet, intelligent woman told me. "People who knew me would always say, 'How could such a good student be unable to find her way?' That made me feel worse."

Ashamed of their inability to find their way, the directionally challenged don't talk about it. When I asked a middle-aged professor how he was treated after people found out he had no sense of direction he said, "Oh, they don't find out. I never tell anyone."

"The only people who know I have no sense of direction," said an attractive special education teacher, "are people I'll never see again—gas station attendants who have given me directions." Since they don't talk about their disability, they have no idea how common it is. Over and over again, in interview after interview I heard people say:

"I thought I was the only one."

"I thought there was something wrong with me."

"Everybody makes fun of me."

"It makes me feel stupid."

"It makes me feel incompetent."

"I don't tell many people."

"Even my kids tease me."

Anything that creates feelings of inferiority in a person is important. And those feelings of inferiority, stupidity, and incompetence often dictate how a person will structure his or her life. Consider the woman who applied to a school of education in order to earn a teaching certificate. She was overjoyed when she was accepted, but when she got her student teaching assignment she pulled out. She was assigned to student teach in a school 30 miles away. "I'll never find it," she said.

"My world could be bigger," said a serious young writer, "It's the directions and the panic."

Many people who lack a good sense of direction are afraid to venture into unknown places. They won't travel alone. They won't join activities that involve driving in unfamiliar places. They are fearful about visiting foreign countries where they might get lost and, because of the language barrier, won't even be able to ask for directions.

My 75-year-old aunt raised four children, works part-time, and is active in her community. Yet she says, "I would never drive a distance by myself in a car. I know I would get lost." Even when she was younger, she told me, she had a terrible time finding her way. She misses many events and skips activities because there is no one to take her, and she won't drive alone. The fear of getting lost is too great.

A friend of mine, a speaker and an author, a dynamic and engaging woman, will not drive on an expressway. "You have to make decisions quickly," she said, and "I won't know which way to go." If she has to travel far, she finds someone to drive her.

Driving is a major hurdle for people with no sense of direction. A young professional woman with two children told me that her life is complicated by the fact that she absolutely refuses to carpool. She takes her children everywhere herself. This is not because she distrusts other parents' driving. She doesn't mind if her children ride with someone else. She just doesn't want other children to ride with her because she is afraid she won't be able to find their homes when it's time to drop them off.

Another woman said, "My husband doesn't understand how tense I am when I get behind the wheel. I feel that I have to know where I am; I don't know for sure, so I get more and more uncomfortable and more and more panicky. He says that if you're going in the right direction, you'll get there. I don't know if I'm going in the right direction. He just can't understand."

"We had just moved to Ann Arbor," said a woman. "My husband wanted me to drop him off at work, leaving me the car to do errands. I didn't want the car. I didn't think I could find my way back home. I was in tears."

The daughter of a successful and well-known physician in answer to the question, "Can your dad drive for the field trip?" will reply, "You don't want to ride with my daddy. He can only get places from our house or from the hospital. If he starts from somewhere else he gets lost."

"I took driver education when I was 16," another woman told me, "but I was so terrified when I realized that I was behind the wheel of a car and didn't know where I was that I quit. I didn't drive again until I was 24."

Cars are trouble for the directionally challenged because they require quick navigation decisions. People who don't know where they are going can't make those decisions right away. They start and stop, trying to decide which way to go. Drivers behind them become angry. They honk. They yell. They make the disoriented driver panic, get angry, or just drive off without knowing the way. "I have to stop at a cross-road and say to myself, 'When I came here did I turn right or left?' If there's a car behind me, I start to feel pressured," said a middle-aged man.

"When I'm driving alone I really concentrate. When I make turns I memorize what's there—landmarks. But it takes a major effort on my part," said a well-known professional in my hometown.

Cars must be parked in safe, visible places. People with no sense of direction often avoid parking in large structures or big surface lots. They're afraid they will not be able to find their car. They will circle streets endlessly until they get a parking space they know they can find again. If they're forced to park in a large lot or parking structure, they might put a bright ribbon on their antenna to make it easy to spot, memorize all the landmarks around the car, or actually draw a picture of the lot marking the spot where their car is parked. Sometimes, if they can't get the "right" spot, they will just go home. I recently attended a family party in New York City. Many of my Michigan relatives flew home on the same plane. After we landed, my husband and I headed for the parking structure to get our car. There we came across my cousin standing in an aisle looking confused. "Did you find it?" he hollered to his wife who was combing the ramp one flight up looking for their car.

"I always park in exactly the same spot when I go to the mall," a young teacher explained. "Otherwise I can't find my car." But parking in the same spot doesn't always help. "If I leave a mall a different way than I entered," an older lady added, "I get confused and can't find my car. I need to call security. They take me around the lot in their truck until I spot something familiar and can get oriented."

People's lives are curtailed because of their fear of getting lost. There are activities they won't join, places they won't go, things they won't do, because they're afraid of getting lost. The fun some people have exploring new places, the sense of adventure that comes with going somewhere new and finding your way, is not a part of their lives.

Are You Directionally Challenged?

What is wrong with those who lack the seventh sense? Headlines announce breakthroughs in gene therapy. Researchers discover new hormones. Once-fatal diseases are controlled. Someone must know why we can't find north.

Little has been written specifically on people with no sense of direction, though some attention has been paid to subjects that touch peripherally on it. There are articles on wayfinding in relation to the design of a building or a park. Psychologists and architects concerned about ease of access have written about the best way to design a hospital, a zoo, or a factory. They write about signage, how many turns to put in a corridor, and making sure there are ways to see outside from inside since this seems to aid in orientation. I was delighted to know that there are architects, landscape designers, and psychologists out there trying hard to keep me from getting lost, but I was not as interested in finding my way as in understanding why I lost my way in the first place.

I found research on cognitive maps quite useful. In their

27

book, *Cognition and Environment,* Michigan psychologists Stephen Kaplan and Rachel Kaplan theorize about how people find their way through their environment. The Kaplans begin by talking about people familiar with their environment. These people know the area so well they don't have to think about directions. They turn the right way automatically.

According to the Kaplans, "a person who is familiar with an environment acts as if there were a model, or a map, of the environment stored in the head." This is called a cognitive map. Considering how large and varied our environment is, the storing of necessary information seems overwhelming.

The idea of a cognitive map was introduced in 1948 by Edward C. Tolman, a psychologist from the University of California at Berkeley. Since then others have come up with different ideas on how the cognitive map works and what it encompasses. Most psychologists who study wayfinding think people depend on a cognitive map consisting of stored information about the environment and associations that connect distinct and separate parts of the environment. If this is so, maybe people who have no sense of direction don't make cognitive maps, make only limited cognitive maps, or can't retrieve information from the cognitive maps they do make.

How would I find out if the people I call "directionally challenged" make cognitive maps? Was it possible to reveal their thinking to learn what they were or were not doing to make them disoriented? One possibility was to find out if those people who said they had no sense of direction shared any other traits.

From the studies I read and reflecting on my own sense of directional deficiency, I developed a list of 22 questions to ask people who claim they lack the seventh sense. I had several things in mind. Besides finding common characteristics, I wanted to know when these people first realized they had a poor sense of direction, if this shortcoming was related to success or failure in subject matters like math and reading, whether they could remember things spatially, and if this disability seemed to run in families. These are the questions. See how they apply to you.

1. When did you realize, and what made you realize, that you were different or that others had a sense of direction and you didn't?

2. How were you treated when people became aware of this deficiency?

3. Do you know of other people in your family who are directionally challenged?

4. When you realized that you had no sense of direction, did you think that was a common problem? Do you think there are many people who are directionally challenged?

5. Can you read a map? Do you like maps? Do you enjoy reading maps?

6. Do you need to have the map facing the way you are going to picture the route and follow the map?

7. Can you automatically reverse directions? In other words, if someone gives you directions to a store, once you're there can you just turn around and go back, or do you have to write the directions backwards?

8. Can you tell left from right?

9. Do you have more trouble finding your way inside a building or outside, navigating through a city? In other words, would you have more trouble finding your way through an

unfamiliar mall or hospital or in an unfamiliar city?

10. Do you use the sun to help you find your way?

11. Do you ever use a compass?

12. Do you remember the location of groups of things? For example, do you remember where the cereals are in a grocery store? If you went in to a new grocery store, one you had never been in before, would you have an idea of how it was set up?

13. Can you picture the layout of your house when you are not in it?

14. If you live in a two-story house and are in a ground floor room can you tell which room is above you?

15. Are you good in language arts?

16. Do you think that you have good verbal skills?

17. Are you good in math?

18. Do you have trouble reading charts and graphs? Do you enjoy reading charts and graphs?

19. Are you claustrophobic?

21. Do you think that if you were more interested, or if you paid more attention, you could be better at finding your way?

22. How do you compensate for this disability?

Common Characteristics— What Do They Mean?

Armed with this questionnaire, I interviewed 25 people, aged 21 to 79—8 men and 17 women. All 25 had claimed to have no sense of direction. On question 1, 10 people realized they were directionally challenged when they began to drive. They had the desire and opportunity to go to distant places, and as teenagers were very anxious for that freedom. But they didn't know how to get anywhere. "I got my license at 16, but from the beginning I never wanted to drive anywhere," said one person. "I always asked someone else. I knew I would get lost."

Worse than their lack of a sense of direction was the embarrassment they felt when they realized they were different. No teenager wants to be different. Some denied their disability; others hid it. One, now 23, when asked how she found her way at 16, said "I got my parents to write directions on little sheets of paper and then I hid them in the glove compartment so no one knew I needed them."

Eight people became aware of their disability when they went to college. They were in unfamiliar surroundings and had difficulty finding their way. At the same time, they noticed that other students seemed to move easily around the campus, taking short cuts to classes, finding new routes to town, and never getting lost. "When I was in college," Betsy told me, "I saw how easily my boyfriend oriented himself. I realized it was instinctive. He had something I didn't have."

The answers to some of the other questions are detailed in figures 1 and 2. I'll summarize them briefly. A large percentage of the people surveyed are good in language arts, fewer are good in math or in chart reading. One wonders whether most people who have no sense of direction tend to be better in language arts and have more trouble in math, but the results don't allow any firm conclusions. It was interesting that very few answered "yes" to question 10, do you use the sun to help you find your way? This makes sense. The sun will tell you which way is east, but if you don't know whether the place you're trying to find is east, west, north, or south, the sun can't help you.

Nearly half of those interviewed have difficulty telling left from right, and more than a third have claustrophobia. These answers may indicate that directional disability is associated with other spatial problems.

The answers to questions 3, (Do you know of other people in your family who are directionally challenged?) 6, (Do you need to have the map facing the way you are going to picture the route and follow the map?) 7, (Can you automatically reverse directions, or do you have to write them in reverse?) and 14 (If you live in a two-story house and are in

Figure 1: Survey results

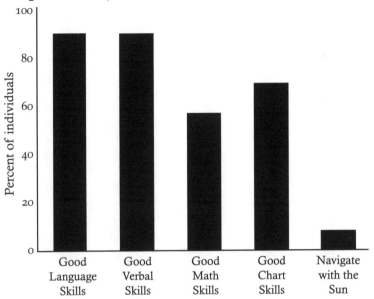

Figure 2: Survey results

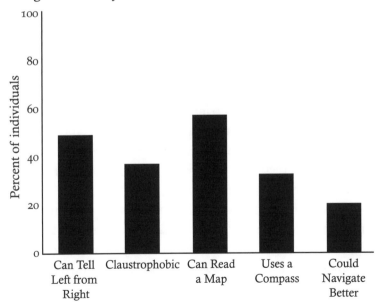

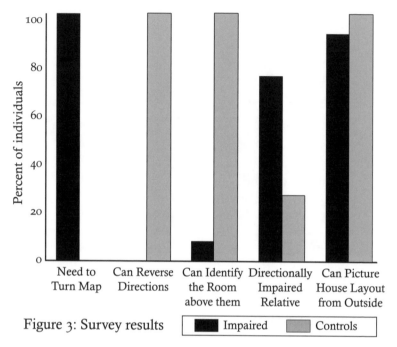

Figure 3: Survey results | ■ Impaired   ■ Controls |

a room on the lower floor of this house, can you tell which room is above you?) stand out because of the consistency of the answers. I was particularly interested in these responses, and therefore recruited a second set of subjects to answer just these questions. This group included 17 individuals—6 men and 11 women—all with an excellent sense of direction. These people served as a comparison group for people with no sense of direction. The answers from both sets of individuals are shown in figure 3.

On question 3, about others in the family, 19 of the 25 directionally challenged people said "yes." This is a much higher percentage than occurred in the 17-member control group of people who had a good sense of direction.

On question 6, about having the map facing the way you are going, only one person could use a map without turning it. In contrast, not one person in the control group needed to turn a map to use it.

In question 7, about reversing directions, none of the 25 challenged persons could do so. They all had to write them down or deliberately force themselves to think consciously about the directions in reverse. All the people in the control group could reverse directions automatically.

Only one person of the 25 directionally challenged interviewed answered "yes" to question 14 about the two-story house. Two others said that if they thought about it for a while they could figure it out. This answer stunned my husband who has an excellent sense of direction. Not being able to identify the room above you was inconceivable to him. When I asked the question to my former business partner, who also has a terrific sense of direction, she was speechless. Finally she asked me if I thought the rooms upstairs moved. All members of the control group could tell which room was above them.

Mulling over these answers, I was bothered by the hypothesis that directionally challenged people don't make cognitive maps. On question 13, picturing the layout of your house when you're not in it, 24 of the 25 directionally challenged people in my survey said yes. That seemed to indicate they had made a cognitive map of their house. I knew that even though I couldn't find my way to and back from many places, it was easy for me to draw a simple layout of the city I lived in. I could picture it in my mind. I had to believe that I had indeed made a type of cognitive map of that city.

There were many places that I could go easily without getting lost, without consciously thinking about where I was. Yet if I was standing in my windowless office, facing the door, I would have no idea which street I was facing. It was as if the outside, not in general but from a specific angle in a specific place, didn't exist if I couldn't see it. I could draw the city, but I couldn't tell you which way I was facing if I couldn't see outside.

A friend suggested that maybe I just had trouble finding my way around enclosed spaces. Maybe if I were outside, I'd have a pretty good sense of direction. Anyone who knows me would immediately discount that idea. I was a tour guide for 14 years; I toured visitors through my city. Before I gave a tour I had to drive along the route and memorize all the turns and all the landmarks. Once I had to give a tour without any preparation and I stood in front of the bus willing away hysteria, praying that the bus driver knew the city well enough to get us to the places I wanted to go. Thank goodness he did. There is no way—inside or out—that I could ever claim to possess even a tiny sense of direction. I could find my way around my office building. I just couldn't picture how my office was situated in relation to the streets around it.

It was another friend who suggested the idea for what I now think is the real reason people don't have a sense of direction. Lynn is a former teacher. She has two daughters, 24 and 26, and was a Girl Scout leader and school volunteer for years. She has a delightful sense of humor and tells wonderful stories about getting lost. One day, in the middle of a discussion about people with no sense of direction, she told me that when she goes shopping at a department store in the large

Ann Arbor mall she has escalator problems. The "up" escalator is on the north side of the store; the "down" escalator is on the south side of the store. She told me that no matter how many times she shops in that store and goes up the "up" escalator and then down the "down" escalator, when she gets back to the first floor she never knows where she is. She can't figure out which way to exit for the parking lot or which way will take her through the store and into the mall. It dawned on me that the reason she became confused was the same reason people couldn't tell which room was above them. She was unable to turn the layout of the store around in her mind. I think I've got it. We, the directionally challenged, are not stupid. We are not crazy. We just can't mentally rotate.

According to psychologists Lynn A. Cooper and Roger N. Shepard, people have the ability to mentally rotate objects. In other words, they can see an object and imagine what it would look like turned 90 or 180 degrees. This mental process of rotation is modeled after the rotation of objects in the physical world. If you can do this, it means that someone can show you a figure shaped a certain way, then show you several other figures, one of which is the original figure rotated so that it is upside down or on its side, etc. You should be able to match the original figure with the figure that is just like it only rotated to a different position. This is something I can't do. When I was in high school we had to take a test that included problems like this. I remember my confusion as I stared at the figures on the paper before me and then looked around the classroom at the other students. They were all busily identifying figures. If anyone besides me was having trouble, I couldn't tell. I was the only one twisting my neck around and around to try and see the figures upside down. I couldn't visualize them turned around.

Try these exercises:

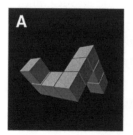
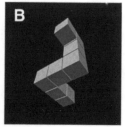
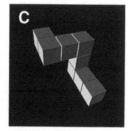

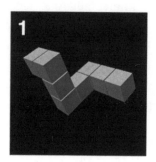

Can you match each of the three figures in the top row to one of the two figures beneath them? Can you do it quickly and easily, or do you have to think a long time?

Answers: A=2, B=1, C=2.

Match the figure at the far left to figure A, B, C, or D in the box.

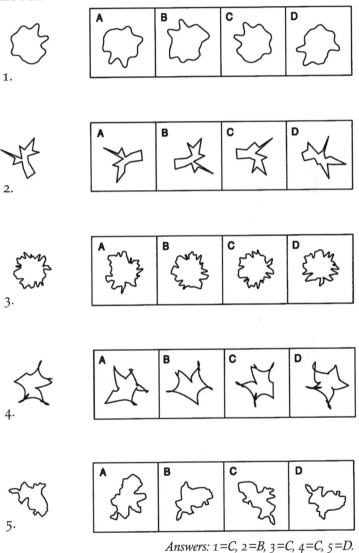

Answers: 1=C, 2=B, 3=C, 4=C, 5=D.

Look at the two rows of figures. Are all the figures in each row the same, just rotated differently, or are some of them different? If some are different, which ones?

Answers: Top row all the same, bottom row F=different.

40

Questions 6, 7, and 14 are patterned along these same lines. Those who have no sense of direction have to turn a map around in their hands because they can't turn it around mentally or can't picture a room overhead because they can't mentally rotate the layout of their home.

Mental Rotation

In their paper, "Turning Something over in the Mind" published in *Scientific American,* December 1984, Lynn Cooper and Roger Shepard explore the question, "What is thinking?" They explain that some thought is verbal, "a kind of silent talking to oneself." Other mental processes, they say, seem to be visual. "Images are called to mind and wordlessly manipulated." People can visualize an object in one position, and then mentally rotate that object to another position. For example, consider moving a card table through a narrow doorway. Cooper and Shepard explained that when asked about this kind of problem, most people picture rotating the table so that two of its legs fit through the door. By turning the table the rest fits through the opening. All this is visualized first to see if it is possible. After the problem is solved mentally, the task is actually undertaken.

To explore the nature of visual manipulation, Cooper and Shepard devised several experiments. The following two tests are like those they created to see if people could actually visualize objects in their mind and then mentally manipulate them.

Mental Rotation—Can You Do It?

Can you match the hands in the top row to the hands in the bottom row without manipulating your own hand to figure out the answer? Just turn the hands around in your mind.

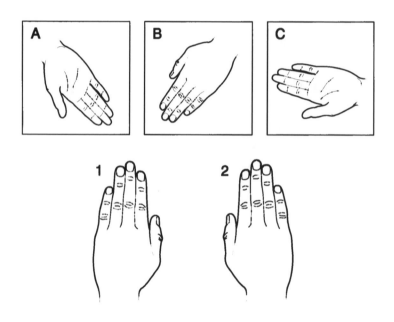

Answers: A=2, B=1, C=1.

Mental Rotation—Who Needs It?

What is the significance of this exercise in everyday life, and how is it connected to people who have no sense of direction? If you are not carrying card tables through narrow doorways, do you need this ability to mentally rotate? Does this ability prevent people from getting lost?

Many scientists, Cooper and Shepard report, have stated that their greatest achievements developed as they imagined and mentally manipulated spatial relations. Albert Einstein said that he arrived at the theory of relativity by "visualizing ... effects, consequences and possibilities through more or less clear images which can be voluntarily reproduced and combined."

If you are a scientist visualization skills are helpful. What about average people not on the verge of great discovery, who are just trying to get through the day? Who uses manipulative visualization? Do people mentally rotate images in their daily lives? The answer is "yes."

Space perception, including the ability to visualize objects in three dimensions and manipulate them to produce a particular configuration, has been shown to be an important skill in occupations that depend on mechanical ability, such as carpentry, plumbing, building, engineering, and auto mechanics. People entering these fields, or thinking about entering them, are often given tests to check their ability to visualize and mentally rotate objects. The Minnesota Paper Formboard Test is a large, standardized test like the SAT, but instead of testing your academic ability it tests your spatial ability. It predicts students' grades in shop and engineering courses as well as supervisors' ratings and production records in inspection, packing, machine operation, and other industrial occupations. Scores on this test are also related to achievement in dentistry and art. The test consists of 64 multiple-choice questions, each with a frame showing a geometric figure divided into several parts, and then five answer frames, each showing a fully assembled form. The subject has to select the one answer frame out of five that shows how the disassembled geometric figure would look if the parts were fitted together. Opposite are two sample questions. Look at the shapes in the upper left hand corner. What would they look like if they were put together? Pick A, B, C, D, or E for your answer.

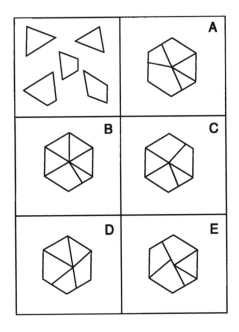

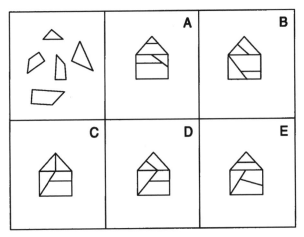

Answers: Top D, bottom D.

Some physicians need the ability to mentally visualize and rotate images of the body. Plastic surgeons, for example, need to be able to picture how a broken or deformed face would look put back together. They need to visualize which bones need to be repositioned for the best results.

A psychiatrist who does not have the ability to visualize or mentally rotate told me that when she was in medical school on the obstetrics service, she had a terrible time delivering a baby because she couldn't picture how the infant was turned as it came through the birth canal, so she didn't know where to put her forceps to help it along.

When she heard this story, a nursing instructor told me she has a terrible time explaining to students the route a baby takes and how it's turned as it travels down the birth canal. The only way she can do it is to stand next to a pregnant woman facing the same direction in which the woman is lying before delivery. For the same reason she can't turn a map around in her mind, she is unable to describe the baby's passage unless she is facing the direction the infant will travel.

An orthodontist with an excellent professional reputation related his troubles in dental school. "I had to work terribly hard to learn to use the mirror," he said referring to the mirror a dentist puts in the patient's mouth. "Everything was reversed," he explained, "and I couldn't mentally turn it around. I went into orthodontics because it's a direct vision thing. I don't need to use a mirror."

A successful decorator with a job in a well-known furniture store said he had a similar problem. When he drew a floor plan he had to keep it facing the same way as the room he was drawing. He also had to keep turning the floor plan as he worked to make sure he would always be facing the right way.

Anyone who has ever bought something unassembled knows how important it is to be able to picture it put together. Figuring out how the directions relate to the materials you are working with can be a problem for people without the ability to visualize and mentally rotate or manipulate. I can remember spending hours trying to put together two drawers. The sales person assured me they were easy to assemble. Thousands of people had bought these drawers, he said, and not one had ever complained about being unable to assemble them. He convinced me that I could easily put together the drawers and also buy shelves and hanging baskets and redo all my closets top to bottom. I left the store feeling wonderful. I was finally going to get organized. I was home by 10 in the morning and couldn't wait to begin. Six hours later I was throwing bolts against the walls, flinging pieces of board around the room, and reduced to tears punctuated by intermittent screams and violent curses. No way could I look at those directions with their cute little drawings and relate them to the drawer I had to put together.

Mental rotation is indeed important in daily life. It can determine your profession, your hobbies, and those chores you can and cannot easily do.

How does this relate to getting lost? In their paper, "Changing Predictors of Map Use in Wayfinding" published in *Developmental Psychology* 1990, Ellen Kofsky Scholnick, Greta G. Fein, and Patricia F. Campbell from the University of Maryland, College Park, say, "Skill in spatial rotation is correlated with skill in map tasks, perhaps because mental rotation helps maintain orientation and map alignment, despite shifts in direction during travel." In other words, those people who have to turn the map in the direction they are going in order to read it, use manual, not mental, rotation. People who can follow directions to an unfamiliar place, but have to consciously reverse the directions in their mind to get back, cannot mentally rotate their route. When people who can't mentally rotate enter a building on the north side and exit on the south side they get confused.

I am not a scientist. I have not done controlled studies to prove that people who are directionally challenged are unable to perform mental rotation. But I have talked to a lot of people with no sense of direction and I believe this is true. Two psychologists who study spatial abilities said they were inclined to agree with me and believe serious study in this area is needed.

Some psychologists dispute the theory that people can mentally rotate images in their mind. Irvin Rock, of the Psychology Department at University of California in Berkeley, in his paper, "Can We Imagine How Objects Look From Other Viewpoints" published in *Cognitive Psychology* 1989, reports the results of several experiments in which subjects try to imagine how three-dimensional objects would appear from other positions. He suggests, after looking at these results, that people don't mentally rotate images at all. Instead, he says, they use other strategies to get the same effect as if they used mental rotation. What does this mean? One way or another, some people can turn visual images around, and some can't. The process really is immaterial. I spoke to people who have a good sense of direction, and asked them to think through the steps they use when reading a map, or when returning from a strange place. They told me they have no conscious idea of what they do. They don't look at a map and think out a strategy for turning the map around in their mind. They simply are able to get from here to there. If psychologists can figure out how people turn things around in their mind they can teach this to the directionally challenged, but it is hard for me to believe that under those circumstances the rotation would proceed as quickly and automatically as it does for those people to whom it comes naturally. There would have to be a conscious step-by-step procedure followed and by the time it was done, you might as well have just turned your map around or written your directions in reverse.

Do Men Get Lost?

Either jokingly or seriously, society tends to focus on women as the ones who always get lost. Yet many men are afflicted with directional disability too. I spoke with over 40 men who do not have a good sense of direction and found they fall into three groups:

Desperate

Desperate men are simply awful at directions and find themselves forced to ask for help because otherwise they'd never get anywhere. Many have wives or colleagues drive them places because they would otherwise get lost. "Did you notice that when we go somewhere I never drive?" said a tall, easygoing physician. "It's easier to let Marilyn do it. Then I don't have to pretend I know where I'm going."

Renaissance

These are the men who have little sense of direction, but are at ease with it and are willing to ask for help if they try to go somewhere and get lost. They are self-confident and don't feel devalued or stupid when they ask for directions. "I finally realized I could ask for directions," said a computer engineer. "I used to think I should be able to do it myself." Some renaissance men are even able to laugh about their disability. When asked how he compensates for his lack of directional sense a friendly, middle-aged man replied, "I married my wife. She has a great sense of direction."

Threatened

Threatened men aren't as directionally challenged as some, but do need help even though they don't always admit it. These men talk about job stress and how their mind is elsewhere so they missed the turn, took the wrong exit, or ended up going north instead of south. They confess that they have always been absent-minded. They allude to the fact that their mind is occupied with larger issues such as wiping out poverty, the existence of God, or how to coordinate all traffic lights, and they don't deal with details like how to get places. Others deny outright that they have any problem finding their way. "I have a good sense of direction," one man told me, incensed that his wife had labeled him directionally disabled. "It's just that she's gifted with maps." Another man told me that since he knows that his wife has a good sense of direction, he just lets her take over. He's learned to depend on her. If he didn't have her around to depend on, he stated, he could find his way just fine himself. "I'm not directionally disabled," he said. "It's just easy to let someone else be in charge of finding the way. It frees me."

"I don't have any trouble finding my way," a farmer said. "It's just that they make the streets wrong. If all the streets were laid out at right angles to all the other streets I would be fine."

"My mother and father used to argue about directions continually," said a friend of my husband. "My father had no sense of direction and couldn't read a map; he turned corners based on intuition. My mother would shove the map under his eyes and say, 'You're supposed to turn here.' He would declare the map wrong and do what he wanted. We were always lost."

Men with no sense of direction suffer embarrassment, often have to depend on others to get places, and sometimes face danger.

"My father has no sense of direction," a young woman told me. "He was in the underground during World War II and his biggest fear was that he would take the wrong path and end up in enemy territory."

A warm, charming woman related a similar story. Her husband fought in World War II, but, even though he was part of the first medical unit across the channel after D-Day, his worst experience was before he was sent overseas. In basic field training, he was given a compass and set down in the middle of nowhere. He had to find his way back. He didn't! They had to come and get him.

Are men generally better than women when it comes to navigation? Or do they just hide their frustration? In an article entitled "Sex Differences in the Brain," published in the September 1992 issue of *Scientific American,* Doreen Kimura, Professor of Psychology at the University of Western Ontario and recipient of the 1992 John Dewan Award for outstanding research from the Ontario Mental Health Foundation, deals with this issue. She found that men and women don't differ in intellectual ability, but they often differ in how well they can perform different functions. Men and women are good at different things. Men, on average, are better able to imagine rotating or manipulating an object than are women. Men also outperform women at navigating their way through a route. Although Dr. Kimura did not link the fact that men are better at mental rotation with the conclusion that men navigate better than women, I suggest that this is the case.

Scientists like Dr. Kimura contend that some abilities are gender based. She cites several of them. Men outperform women on mathematical reasoning tests. They are more accurate in tests of target-directed motor skills like throwing a football, and they are better at navigating their way through a route. Women are better than men at identifying matching items. They have greater verbal fluency and outperform men in arithmetic calculation. They remember landmarks on a route better than men do.

Most people doing psychological research believe that hormones influence gender-based ability and behavior. Differing patterns of ability and behavior, according to Dr. Kimura, probably reflect different hormonal influences on the developing male and female brain. Many studies done with rats show this to be true. For example, Kimura cites a study in which a rodent with functioning male genitals is deprived of male hormones, including testosterone, immediately after birth. Male sexual behavior in this rodent was reduced. Instead, female sexual behavior developed. The reverse is also true. If androgens—male sex hormones—are given to a female rodent directly after birth, she will display more male sexual behavior and less female sexual behavior.

According to Dr. Kimura, the effect of early exposure to sex hormones appears to alter brain function permanently and affect not only sexual behavior, but all behavior in which most males and females tend to differ. Giving the hormones at a later time in development does not have this effect. Studies of girls who were exposed to excess male sex hormones in the prenatal or neonatal stage seem to support this finding.

Sheri A. Berenbaum of the University of Chicago and Melissa Hines of the University of California at Los Angeles observed the play behavior of these girls and compared it to that of their male and female siblings. When given a choice of dolls and kitchen supplies, books and board games, or transportation and construction toys, these girls with excess androgens chose to play with what we would consider the more typically male transportation and construction toys. They played with cars for the same amount of time boys did. Susan M. Resnick at the National Institute on Aging, Sheri A. Berenbaum, and their colleagues also reported that these girls were superior to their unaffected sisters in one spatial manipulation test and two spatial rotation tests. Men usually perform better than women on these tests. Though the number of girls studied by Resnick and Berenbaum is small, their conclusions suggest that early exposure to sex hormones may influence male and female spatial abilities, specifically, mental rotation, as well as other male and female behavior. This and many other solid research studies support the concept that higher testosterone levels during fetal development play a part in promoting the development of the part of the brain responsible for mental rotation. Therefore men, whose brains are exposed to more testosterone during development, have a better ability to mentally rotate. If a good sense of direction is dependent on the ability to mentally rotate, as I believe it is, more men will have a better sense of direction than women.

Dr. Kimura, along with others in her field, has speculated that this effect of male hormones may be attributable to evolution. I was first introduced to evolutionary theory by my physician husband. He advanced this idea to account for the better wayfinding ability men seem to possess. "I bet this is due to natural selection," he told me. "Ages ago, men were the hunters. It was their job to go out into the wilds, find game, kill it, and bring it home. If they weren't successful, their families didn't eat. A directionally challenged male in primitive societies would die. He would set out through the woods to kill a deer and never find his way back home. Consequently, males with a good sense of direction survived. Their genes were passed on."

"The women in early societies stayed near home. They prepared the food and cared for the children. They didn't need a good sense of direction because they didn't go anywhere."

Dr. Kimura proposes something similar in a more sophisticated manner. She suggests that genes responsive to testosterone were preserved because they were necessary for survival. Society needed men who could hunt and not get lost. If their genes were not responsive to testosterone, they were unable to hunt successfully and their genes were not passed on.

But what about the fact that some men are better than others at finding their way and some women are very good at wayfinding? There are differences in directional ability between men as a group and between women as a group as well as between individual men and women. This is probably due to the influence of factors other than, and in addition to, hormones acting on the brain. There seems to be a strong genetic factor involved. My surveys show a tendency for directional disability to run in families.

Further research in these areas is needed before definitive conclusions can be reached. The research that has been done suggests that our ability to remain oriented, to navigate, or find our way is based not on how much we pay attention, not on how smart we are, but perhaps on a combination of genetic and other factors including the way sex hormones act upon our brain. Hopefully future studies will give us a better picture of this fascinating view of directional disability.

Children Get Lost, Too

How many times have you heard a store employee announcing a lost child over the public address system? How many times have you seen a small child in tears unable to find his mother? How often have you bent down to hear a little one say, "I'm lost."? If we accept either the fact that the ability to perform certain spatial tasks such as mental rotation stems from the action of hormones on our brain (before or immediately after birth) or has something to do with genes and natural selection, it is not surprising that young children exhibit either a good or bad sense of direction. Kimberly A. Kerns, working with Sheri Berenbaum at the University of Chicago, found that sex differences in spatial rotation performance are present before puberty.

Four- and five-year-old children have been studied to evaluate their map reading and wayfinding abilities. In their article, "Changing Predictors of Map Use in Wayfinding," published in the 1990 issue of *Developmental Psychology,* Ellin Kofsky Scholnick, Greta G. Fein, and Patricia F. Campbell found that for younger children, the ability to mentally rotate was a major predictor of how well a child was able to use a map.

In our family, wayfinding skill, or lack thereof, was evident at an early age. My daughter recalls sitting in her kindergarten class trying to be invisible when the teacher asked for volunteers to take the attendance slip to the office. Hands waved, bodies wiggled as the kids tried to get the teacher's attention, hoping to be picked. My daughter's hand didn't wave. Her body didn't wiggle. She was afraid to be picked. She knew she would wander the halls frightened, unable to find the office. And if she did, by some chance, find the office she would still have had to figure out how to get back to her class.

In my school library classes, children in kindergarten and first grade will often ask permission to go to the bathroom or get a drink. When I tell a child to go ahead, it's not unusual for that child to come up to me and say quietly, "I don't know where the bathroom is." There is a bathroom located very close to the library. It is not enough, however, to tell the child to go a few steps down the hall and he will find the bathroom. He'll stand at the library door looking bewildered and then come back in and say, "I don't know how to get there." Someone will have to go with him. The same thing happens when a child tells me that she has left a library book in her classroom. If I say go get it, the majority of children will do that, but every once in a while a child will say, "I don't know how to get back to the classroom."

It's interesting to observe young children's behavior when their class leaves the library. The routine requires lining up at the library door with a teacher in front. The class then leaves the library together and walks in a line down the hall to their classroom. Often children are still checking out a book when their class is ready to leave. The class leaves on time and the remaining children check out their books and follow. Some children panic when this happens, especially if it looks as though they will be the only one from their class left in the library. They beg someone to wait for them or they say they can't check out their book because the class is leaving and then run as fast as they can to catch up with the line of students. I suspect these are the children who can't find their way back to the classroom alone.

"It's easy to tell who is directionally challenged," a second grade teacher told me. "They're the ones you send on an errand and don't see again. They are found much later, alone in a hallway, totally disoriented."

"When I was in the third grade," said a prominent physician, "we moved to a new place. I could walk to school. My first day at the new school I left from the wrong end of the playground. I was just one and a half blocks from my house, but I got turned around and couldn't find my way home. I had to return to school and begin again." This man is now 54, and his sense of direction has not improved.

"I remember when I was about 10 or 12 and my mother went into a bank to do an errand leaving me outside with my sister," a pretty writer told me. "It seemed like a long time and my mother wasn't back. I suddenly realized that I didn't know how to get home. It was a very scary feeling." This same writer, now in her 50s, loves to travel, but if she is anywhere outside her neighborhood she doesn't have a clue as to how to get home.

"I started high school," a middle-aged man revealed, "and I realized I was having trouble navigating through the corridors. I never knew where I would end up."

"In high school I couldn't find the lunchroom. I had to hope the people I was following were going there."

"My son ran track in school," a mother informed me. "He was running down the main street of our suburb with his teammates. He fell behind. The others turned a corner. When he got there they were out of sight. He didn't know how to get back to school. He had to call me to pick him up." He still has no sense of direction, but has learned to compensate and gets along very well.

Some children are like homing pigeons. They can get home from anywhere and often direct adults. Others seem anchorless, small lost objects in huge spaces. They have no idea where they are, not because they are young, but because they have no sense of direction. Most of them don't realize how they differ from their friends. It is these children who grow up to be directionally challenged adults.

The reason we don't think about children getting lost is because a sense of direction is, for the most part, not important for them. They are taken most places. Parents drive them to school or put them on a school bus. If they walk to school, for safety's sake they usually walk in a group. Children are encouraged to play near their home. They are not sent long distances by themselves. As one man said to me, "When you're a kid, there's always some adult that you follow." So it is not surprising that when you ask people to name the time they first realized they lacked a sense of direction, the answer is not second grade but when they learned to drive. That was the first time most of them were asked to go somewhere far away from their neighborhood alone.

"Even though I got my driver's license, I didn't want to drive," a teacher recalled. "I knew I would get lost. I always asked someone else to take me."

"As soon as I started to drive I realized I had no sense of direction. I was terrified to drive on an expressway because I never knew where I was when I got off."

"I realized that I didn't have a sense of direction when I started driving and suddenly it was *my* responsibility to get somewhere, not my parents," a young woman told me. "I was always late to things because I couldn't find my way. My friends used to tell me an event started earlier than it really did because they knew I would get lost and be late."

A driver's license means freedom and independence to some; to others it means anxiety and fear.

What can parents do to help? If I had known my daughter was directionally challenged, I would have done things differently. On every walk we took around the block, through the woods, to the drugstore, I would have pointed out landmarks, just to get her used to looking at her surroundings and remembering them. For the directionally challenged, much wayfinding depends on observation and memorization.

I would have talked more openly about my inability to find my way and how I cope instead of trying to hide it and appear always in control. If your child sees that you can't do something and it's ok, he or she will adopt the same accepting attitude. Hopefully a loss of self-esteem can be prevented.

Especially when my daughter was in elementary school,

I would have informed teachers of her inability to find her way. Much anxiety could have been avoided if kindergarten and first grade teachers had not sent her alone on errands in different parts of the school. It's just as easy to tell two children to take the attendance slip to the office or deliver a note to the gym teacher. More children would then get a turn to feel important, and the directionally challenged child would be able to avoid embarrassment.

What else can you do to help a child who is easily disoriented? Two colleagues of mine discussed this. Margie said that after her daughter learned to drive she just let her go. She figured it was important to give her as much experience finding her way as possible. Now she has a great sense of direction. "Doesn't matter," replied Judy. "I did the same thing with both my daughters, but one is like me—she can't get anywhere—and the other one always knows where she is. Since childhood she has been the one to tell everyone how to get places."

Robin Moore, an expert in playground design at North Carolina State University, suggests encouraging your child to play outside. In an article on the value of playing outside that appeared in the March 8, 1998 *Detroit Free Press,* she says that as children get older, around 8 or 10, they need to have a sense of ownership of their own territory. This may be important, she states, for developing a child's understanding of spatial relationships and sense of direction.

If you accept the idea that people who are directionally challenged cannot perform mental rotation, you realize that there are many things children are asked to do in school that may be difficult for a child with no sense of direction. In art, that child may be able to draw an object in front of him as it appears, but he may not be able to draw that object from the side or turned around. Mirror images might be hard for these children, but they might excel in sculpture, since you can walk around the piece you sculpt and see it from all sides.

In science, a child may be able to memorize the growth rings of a tree, but if you show her a cross section or a slide of those rings and expect her to put it in context, you might be expecting the impossible.

In social studies, a globe is a better teaching tool than a map. Some children have trouble looking at a flat map and picturing the way countries on the east side of the map connect with the countries on its west side.

According to Dr. Sharon Muir, Professor of Education at Oakland University in Detroit, children with some spatial disabilities learn mapping skills and directions more easily if their desks are placed facing north, providing a visible point of reference.

Cutting out pictures and shapes of countries and having children arrange them in proper order makes it easier for them to learn where each country is in relation to the others. Children can use their hands to help them learn.

In math, also, manipulatives are important, especially for teaching geometrical concepts. For children who can't mentally rotate figures, manual rotation makes learning easier. "I always use manipulatives," said an elementary school teacher. "They help children who can't picture things in their minds."

It's important that teachers be made aware at parent-teacher conferences or during informal conversations that they may have to utilize different teaching methods with the directionally challenged child. Certainly every school of education should, along with making their students aware that children learn in different ways, provide them with specific methods for teaching the child with spatial challenges. Subjects that are difficult for these children should be identified. Children should not be humiliated or made to feel stupid because they are unable to learn the same way others can. Talk to a group of directionally challenged adults and you will hear sad school stories. Here are seven examples:

⇨ "I took an IQ test when I was young and I did exceptionally well in everything but the section on spatial skills, particularly the part that included mental rotation. They pulled me out of class and made me repeat that part of the test because they couldn't believe I was smart and couldn't do it," a poised and obviously intelligent woman related.

⇨ "As a child math was hard for me. I couldn't visualize what was going on. I would memorize all the examples, but not understand the principle behind them. Now I teach it to second graders," said an intense elementary school teacher. "When I teach it I use lots of manipulatives so I can see and understand what I'm saying and so my kids can see and understand it, too."

⇨ "Anything with spatial relationships is hard for me, like mentally flipping figures and imagining the other side," added another teacher.

⇨ "I couldn't do solid geometry because I couldn't picture the figures," another person told me.

⇒ "I wanted to take geology in college, but I couldn't look at cross sections and figure them out," said a tall, middle-aged woman. "I decided not to risk it."

⇒ "I thought about going into medicine, but I didn't do very well in anatomy. I could memorize all the bones and muscles and I could draw whatever I could see," an energetic young mother explained. "But I couldn't figure out what they were showing when they took a slice of this or that."

⇒ "Organic chemistry was very hard for me; I couldn't mentally rotate the compounds to see how they interact," a physician friend told me.

By the time my daughter learned to drive it was too late for me to give her tips on finding her way. The last thing a 16-year-old wants is advice from her mother, especially if it suggests that she is different from her peers. But I could have prepared her. When we went places I could have shown her my directions and asked her to help me look for landmarks on the way. Hopefully this would have gotten her in the habit of looking for landmarks herself. I could have made sure she knew I always took the name and phone number of my destination in case I needed to call for additional directions. I would have let her know that I didn't consider this embarrassing and that lots of other people did the same thing.

When we drove to familiar places she would need to know how to locate—the mall, the grocery, the school—I should have commented aloud as were going, "I have to remember to turn right at the gas station," or " I always know where to turn to get to the grocery because there is a big white church on the corner." Gradually she would have absorbed the clues she would need in the future. A directionally challenged woman agreed with me. She explained that her son had no sense of direction and what seemed to help him was a picture of the city layout. Her husband would make picture maps for him to look at.

Finally, I wish I would have verbally addressed the problem of getting lost in a relaxed fashion. "If we get lost we can always stop and call, ask at a gas station, or look at a map. If we get lost we can just look for that large water tower, then we'll know where we are." I would have liked to foster a "no big deal" attitude. Fear is a bigger road block than lack of a sense of direction.

Drivers training teachers could help the directionally challenged child. As part of their course, they could include tips for finding your way and a section on what to do if you get lost. This would be for everybody making sure certain children aren't singled out. There could even be some instruction in map reading. While children have had to use maps to find states and countries in school classes, few have had much experience reading road maps.

Good maps, in addition to written directions, could be helpful to many children. The two times my children changed schools, matriculating from elementary to middle school and from middle to high school, I took them to their new school in advance of opening day. Together we found their locker, the lunchroom, and the bathroom. We received their class schedule and found all their classrooms. It would have been helpful, however, if each child entering a new school was given a map, along with written directions, including land-marks, to the places he or she would have to go. Directions to the gym, the lunchroom, the general office, the auditorium, for example, would be needed by all.

Inevitably some children will have a good sense of direction, others will not. With some thought and planning we can make life easier for those who won't.

Medical Students
and Directional Disability

"How is the book coming?" one of my husband's colleagues inquired. "I just learned something very interesting," I replied. I had interviewed several people with no sense of direction who considered going to medical school, but couldn't understand cross sections and were afraid they wouldn't be able to pass anatomy. They couldn't picture how the pieces fit into the whole. Since this physician was both directionally challenged and a superb doctor, a molecular biologist known throughout the medical community for his research, I asked if he had any trouble with anatomy in medical school. "I almost failed it," he answered. I was stunned. This was one brilliant man, yet he had a terrible time understanding cross sections. His comment made my research come to life. I told him about my medical student study.

My husband, a medical school faculty member, told me that the faculty committee reviewing student performance discussed two students failing anatomy and struggling with histology (microscopic anatomy). One of the professors said he thought some students in histology couldn't visualize three-dimensional structures. In this class, students examine a tissue cross section to identify what the whole tissue looks like. At the time, I was interviewing people for this book and many of our dinner conversations revolved around what people without a sense of direction could and couldn't do. I had just spoken with several directionally challenged people who said they had trouble understanding cross sections. My husband speculated that the students in question might be directionally challenged, and a study was born.

These surveys were sent to all first- and second-year medical students at the University of Michigan Medical School.

Do you think you have a good sense of direction?

☐ yes   ☐ no

IF NOT,
When did you realize you lack a good sense of direction?

_____

_____

_____

_____

Do you use a map to find your way?

☐ yes   ☐ no

If you use a map, do you need to turn it in the direction you are going to use it?   ☐ yes   ☐ no

If you are given directions from your home to an unfamiliar place, and you follow them and get there, can you get back to your home automatically, without thinking about it? ☐ yes ☐ no

OR

Do you have to either write the original directions backwards, or consciously think, "I turned right at this corner, so I need to turn left here to get home."

☐ yes ☐ no

If you live in a two-story house, can you sit in a room on the first floor and identify the room above you?

☐ yes ☐ no

Do you have trouble understanding cross sections?

☐ yes ☐ no

Are you able to look at directions and easily assemble something? ☐ yes ☐ no

Do you know anyone in your family who is directionally challenged? ☐ yes ☐ no

How do you compensate for this disability?

_____

_____

_____

_____

One hundred twenty-six surveys were returned. Twenty-seven out of 126 students (22 percent) said they did not have a good sense of direction. Of those 27, 13 (48 percent) had trouble understanding cross sections. In comparison, of the 99 who said they did have a good sense of direction, only 9 (10 percent) had trouble with cross sections. The likelihood of this happening by chance alone is less than one in 10,000. There is a highly significant difference between the ability to do cross sections among those with a good sense of direction and those with a bad sense of direction. Since this study showed people without a good sense of direction have trouble with cross sections we wanted to know if this handicapped them in medical school.

Learning anatomy, histology, and embryology—three very important courses for medical students—requires understanding cross sections. We looked at the grades of the medical students who responded to the survey. Great news! The grades of the students who identified themselves as having a poor sense of direction were just as high as the grades of the students who said they had a good sense of direction. We may be chronically lost, but that shouldn't stop us from becoming doctors.

Since a larger percentage of directionally challenged students have trouble with cross sections, why aren't their grades worse? Have they learned to work harder? Are they better students to begin with? Do they have a method for coping ? We don't know. Somehow they were able to overcome their disability.

An interesting fact appeared as we analyzed the data further. We found that students who cannot reverse directions do significantly worse in anatomy, compared to their performance in their other courses, than students who can reverse directions easily. Apparently a student's ability to easily reverse directions predicts how well he or she will do in anatomy. Of the students who said they had a poor sense of direction, only one of 27 was able to reverse directions. But 31 out of the 99 students who said they had a good sense of direction couldn't reverse directions. This made me reflect on the definition of sense of direction. Perhaps those 31 students who said they had good navigational skills but couldn't reverse directions were able to use a map or follow directions. However they may not have had that intuitive sense of where they are that characterizes people I define as having a good sense of direction. More research needs to be done.

Sex is always interesting, and that holds true in these survey results. More women than men reported having a poor sense of direction. Thirty-two percent of the women who returned the survey said they had a poor sense of direction while just 12 percent of the men said they had a poor sense of direction. That is statistically highly significant, very unlikely to happen by chance alone. Only 5 percent of the men had trouble with cross sections, compared with 31 percent of the women. A total of 33 percent of the men had trouble reversing directions compared with 59 percent of the women. Medical students may often seem to be a breed apart, but in this survey they were just like the general population. More women than men appear to have certain spatial difficulties. It should be noted, however, that these women are pushing on despite their disabilities. Yes to the strong, tough women who, like their mothers and grandmothers, have learned to cope in the face of adversity.

Despite the ambiguity in some of the survey results, they were fun to read and reinforced many of my findings on the directionally challenged. For example, some students noticed their directional disability at a young age. Answers to the question about when they realized they lacked a good sense of direction included the following:

"In fourth grade, when I moved to a different state and got lost walking home from school."

"I was a child. There was terror when I couldn't figure out how to get to the next level of a store."

"From the time I was very young I got lost whenever I tried to go anywhere I didn't know well."

"When I moved to a new town (age 14) and had to use the bus system to get to my new school across town."

"Age 10, ever since I needed to find places—to go by my-self—I always got lost."

A large percentage of these students realized they had a poor sense of direction when they learned to drive. But others noticed their lack of a directional sense when they were somewhat older.

"When I realized my friends can reference themselves to a map by understanding 'this direction is north.'"

"When I realized that getting directions such as east, west ... never help me and streets that curve immediately mess up what direction I think I'm going in."

"When people give directions and say, 'Go north at the light.'"

"About 7 or 8 years ago when it was pointed out to me that when I am indoors (in my own house) I point in a random direction when talking about outside destinations like a street, or neighboring town, etc., and that not everyone does that."

"Just recently in conversations with my wife."

As I read more comments I realized that these students were just like me.

"After five years of living in Ann Arbor I still can't find my way through the mall."

"It's hard for me to visualize some of the tricky intersections when streets curve."

"I noticed that I couldn't turn things in my head."

"In ninth grade during geometry class I had trouble picturing and drawing 3-D objects."

Medical students are thought to be smart, highly motivated achievers. There probably aren't many things they find difficult. I wondered if they had trouble accepting the fact that there were some things they simply couldn't do. I wanted to talk to them, find out what they were like, but these surveys were anonymous.

Celebrities Get Lost

In her warm and witty way, Ann Landers has an answer for every problem. Thousands of people write to her for advice. Many of them have no sense of direction. Confused and uncertain, they explain that they are active, intelligent people, normal in every way except that no matter how hard they try, they can't find their way. "They think they are crazy," Ms. Landers said. All she can do is assure them that they are not crazy and they are not alone. She should know. Ann Landers has no sense of direction herself. In one of her columns she admitted, "I can't find my way out of a phone booth." When I spoke to her I asked if she used a map to find her way. "I don't have anything to do with maps," she stated in a tart Iowa twang. "I always have somebody with me. I have a driver. I haven't driven in 30 years." Her directional disability certainly hasn't stopped her. Even though Ann Landers claims that when traveling she never turns the right way out of her hotel room, she *has* been able to navigate through the world with humor and wisdom dispensing help and hope in a generous and sensible way.

Ken and Margie Blanchard are consultants, specialists in efficient organizational management. Together they founded Blanchard Training and Development Inc., a human resource development company. Dr. Blanchard wrote *The One Minute Manager*, and he and his wife are noted experts in business management and human resources. Not much comes along that they can't handle. Yet when I spoke to Ken Blanchard he had just gotten lost driving to his son's house. He said, with no sense of embarrassment, that he had a poor sense of direction. He was in a meeting when I called and asked if he could phone back. The next day his voice boomed over the phone, sounding warm and comfortable. "Margie said to tell you she has a worse sense of direction than I do. She wants to know if she's famous enough to be included in your book."

Beverly Sills has held audiences spellbound. She first stepped on stage at age 3 and has been on and around stages ever since. In the 1960s, for many, opera was Beverly Sills. Looking at her, one would never suspect this former manager of the New York City Opera and chairwoman of Lincoln Center would ever become hopelessly lost. Yet, according to this interview and story by Ralph Blumenthal that appeared in the February 13, 1996 *New York Times,* Sills is directionally challenged. He wrote:

> Somewhere under Lincoln Center for the Performing Arts, Beverly Sills is lost. Upstairs in Avery Fisher Hall, a German film crew is waiting to interview her for a 70th birthday tribute to Kurt Masur, the New York Philharmonic's music director, who is to present her on camera with a hand-carved Bohemian Nutcracker.

But on this recent Friday morning, Ms. Sills—who has worked around the plaza for 30 years as reigning diva, then manager of the New York City Opera and, since 1994, as chairwoman of Lincoln Center—can't find the underground passage to the orchestra's stage door. Finally she plows outside into a rain squall, renegotiates the labyrinth and is rewarded upstairs with an effusive bear hug from the towering maestro.

Ms. Sills, who is 66 years old, may never quite figure out her way around the sprawling complex—'I don't have a sense of direction,' she admits—but that hasn't prevented her from putting her imprint on the world's largest performing arts center.

Who would know more about being challenged than Florine Mark, president and CEO of Weight Watchers in Michigan? As a young woman, she struggled with her weight, trying diet after diet. Using Weight Watchers she lost 50 pounds and has kept it off for 30 years. With determination and persistence she helped herself, and then went on to help people worldwide lose weight and become happier, healthier and more self-confident.

"When I was a teenager," she said, "I took the bus everywhere. I didn't think about a sense of direction until I was older." At the time, Mark lived in Palmer Woods, a lovely area of Detroit with big trees and beautiful winding streets. "It's confusing in there," she explained. "I'd take a walk and get lost. I'd knock on a neighbor's door and say, 'Where am I?' I began memorizing landmarks in the area so I could get back home." How do you get around now? I asked her. "I don't drive myself. I was a mother of five. I had all the responsibilities. One day I sat down and made a list of what I could depend on others for—driving! What a sense of relief, since I never know where I'm going."

How do you feel about being directionally challenged I asked her? "I think you have to have a sense of humor about it. Laugh, have fun. I don't like panic or being frightened so I joke a lot about it."

When I asked permission to include Mark in this book, she replied with her typical warmth, "If I can help one person to realize it's ok not to be perfect, that's great." Though she hadn't heard my views on mental rotation and spatial disabilities, Mark, sensible and down-to-earth, ended our interview with this: "Saying to a person with no sense of direction, 'If you'd only pay attention you could find your way,' is like saying to a person who is overweight, 'Just stop eating and you'll be fine.'"

Joan Baez was signing CDs at a Borders Bookstore near my home. "What a perfect opportunity," I thought, "to find out if she is directionally challenged." I ran down to the bookstore hoping there was no line, that no one remembered Joan Baez. No chance. In Ann Arbor, home of the '60s revolutionaries, every aging civil rights activist was in line.

"What does she look like?"

"How old could she be?"

"Do you remember?"

"Do you remember?"

"Do you remember?"

And, of course, we all remembered.

When I got to the head of the line, I could see that she looked great. She had the same beautiful, interesting face, warm, intelligent eyes, and now short, gray hair. She wore pants, a shirt, and a stunning long scarf over her shoulder. Sophisticated, at ease, she spoke to each person, never rushing, always courteous. When my turn came, I asked her if she had a good sense of direction. She looked at me as though I had come out of left field and began to laugh. "I have a perfectly terrible sense of direction," she replied. "Why do you want to know?" "Another one, yes!" I said to myself as she spoke of never knowing where she was. She pointed out her tour manager and told me that he takes her everywhere she needs to go. She said she would be happy to be in my book.

"What about that guy who got lost going to an Atlanta Braves game?" a friend asked when I told him I was looking for famous lost people. "What guy?" My friend couldn't remember.

I called the P.R. man for the Atlanta Braves. "Oh yeah," said Glen Ferra. "Pasqual Perez. The story's all true. He'd just gotten his driver's license I think. I don't even know how much English he spoke. He got on the highway that goes around the perimeter of the city. He went around the 38-mile perimeter three times looking for the stadium. Then he ran out of gas. I don't remember how he finally got there—a cab, hitchhiked—but he was too late to pitch. We were in the middle of a losing streak. Everyone was tense, but when he got there and the players heard the story, they laughed so much the guys loosened up." It might have been a turning point. "After that," he continued, "we won 13 out of 15 and won the division."

Ferra laughed telling the story, but then admitted that he too had no sense of direction. "Some of those ballparks," he said, "I've been there a hundred times. But I'll make a wrong turn coming out and I'm lost. When you go somewhere, it's the getting back. I can't reverse it. Like I have to say I turned right going in so I have to turn left going out. My wife's the navigator."

How You Can Compensate

The most amazing thing about the directionally challenged is the way they bond when they're brought together. At parties and meetings, in classrooms and workplaces, when the subject of directional ability is raised, those who lack a sense of direction congregate in small groups and share stories. Listening to their experiences, you can sense the comfort they feel in knowing that they are not the only ones who can't find their way out of malls and lose their cars in parking lots. One person will start a story and by the time he or she has the first few words out people are already nodding, not with their usual embarrassment, but with the enthusiasm felt when you sense someone is just like you. Suddenly, in this group, you are just like everyone else.

What a relief not to feel different. And the directionally challenged feel different. We are uncomfortable admitting we're afraid of getting lost. We feel as if we are the only ones who can't cope. We know we should be able to find our way. It seems as if everybody else can. Yet when we have to go to a strange place, we get nervous and upset. We get angry that this seems so difficult. Most of all we feel helpless. We have to get somewhere, but we are afraid to go. And even if we do take the bull by the horns and just do it, we do it with knots in our stomach, sweat on our hands, and tears in our eyes.

What can be done to alleviate some of this tension? Discussions with the directionally challenged reveal that they can and do compensate.

A sales representative keeps a notebook in his car. Every time he has to go someplace new, he writes down directions, landmarks to watch for, mileage, and other details.

"That's what I do," said a lovely, middle-aged woman when I told her about the notebook. "I keep index cards with directions to different places I go all the time. I have notebooks of directions for the major cities we visit frequently. One of my major accomplishments was learning to read a map. I have a neighborhood map by my phone. If I have to call a cab I can tell the driver how to get here." She went on to say that her daughter was also directionally challenged. "When she comes home from California, where she goes to school," the mother explained, "I put index cards in her room with directions to the mall, friends' houses and other places she may want to go. I know she won't remember how to get there."

"Keep a tape recorder in the car," one woman suggested. "When you go someplace new, turn on the tape and record all the turns and all the significant landmarks. Before you go home, play the tape and review the directions."

"I have my husband look at the map and figure out where I have to go. Then he writes down directions for me, two sets, one there and one back."

"If it's important that I get someplace on time I practice the day before," a friend told me. "I drive the route till I'm sure I know it and then I feel comfortable the next day when I have to do it for real."

"Don't give up," a young accountant said. "I have a high tolerance for turning down streets and continuing until I see something I know."

"I use all the Boy Scout tricks," a neighbor said. "I wear a watch with a compass on it. I read a map. I look at the sun. I've been known to search for the moss on a tree."

"Planning, planning, planning," said a pretty executive.

"I think it must be really hard for people who aren't compulsive, who just want to wing it," a tall, graceful woman speculated. "I couldn't compensate if I wasn't willing to spend the extra time preparing to go somewhere, write out directions, note landmarks, draw maps."

Remember that there's nothing shameful about getting lost. Lost people are not mean people or bad people or dishonest people. They're just lost. Work on accepting yourself. When asked to describe people who seek directions, gas station attendants, salespeople in convenience stores, policemen, use one word, embarrassed.

"I learned that I simply had to get past the embarrassment and admit that I couldn't find my way," a young man said. "If I'm driving with someone else I give up control and let them take over."

"Ask directions. In the last 10 years," a man told me, "I realized that it was ok to ask. I used to think I should be able to figure everything out by myself. Now I feel all right about asking."

Here are some more tips from those in the know.

When Driving to an Unfamiliar Place

⇨ Get clear, specific directions with mileage and landmarks included.

⇨ Have someone draw you a simple picture of how to get there.

⇨ Learn to read a map, even if you have to turn it to use it.

⇨ Highlight your route on the map so you won't have to search for it.

⇨ Ask directions, and keep asking every few miles if necessary.

⇨ Carry a car phone so you can always call and ask directions.

⇨ Never leave late. Allow time to get lost.

When Parking in a Large Lot or Garage

⇨ Never park and hurry away. Always take time to look around and line up your car with a landmark you can find again.

⇨ Take note of all the signs and markers near your car.

⇨ Draw a picture of your car and all the things around it before you leave the area.

⇨ Remember where you exit.

⇨ Figure out a way to identify your exit. Is it next to a large tree, a big trash container, or a street light?

⇨ Tie a ribbon or a flower on your antenna to make your car easier to see.

When Walking through a Strange City

⇨ Look at a map and pick out the main streets. Memorize them.

⇨ Find the streets that run parallel to the main streets. Remember their names.

⇨ See if the streets are arranged in a pattern that will help you.

⇨ Carry a notebook with you. As you walk, jot down the landmarks you pass in the order they occur.

⇨ If you have a destination in mind and are not just meandering, time yourself. That way you'll know about how long it should take you to return.

⇨ Look at the street signs. Silently say the names of the streets you pass to fix them in your memory.

⇨ If you enter a building, figure out some way of identifying the entrance you used. Always go out the same way you came in.

Anytime—Things to Remember

⇨ Don't panic! Don't panic! Don't panic!

⇨ People who get lost get found.

⇨ Ask directions. Most people are friendly and helpful and will be glad to show you the way.

⇨ Practice wayfinding. Go someplace in your town, not

too far from your home, that you have never been before. Plan a route in advance. Do this several times a month, gradually going further and further afield. The more you venture out alone, the better you'll get and the more comfortable you'll feel.

⇒ Keep a positive attitude. Even those people who were afraid to venture to new places alone said that it was important to have the right attitude. You can't be afraid to get lost. People with no sense of direction who are afraid of getting lost never go anywhere. Keep thinking that getting lost is not a big deal. You just find yourself and then carry on. People who accept the fact that they may get lost and treat it as just a small annoyance deal best with their lack of a seventh sense.

What Changes
Should Be Instituted?

There are many things people who are directionally challenged can do to make their lives easier. There are also
things we as a society can do to make wayfinding simpler on
highways and city streets, in shopping malls and parking lots,
at airports and office complexes. Color coding, inside landmarks, numbered or lettered areas, windows, three-dimensional
maps, good signage, and car navigational devices can help the
directionally challenged find their way.

Office complexes, shopping malls, airports, hospitals, and
parking structures should all be color coded. If each area was
painted a different color, and a map was provided describing
each colored area, people could easily see their destination.

Large indoor areas should have landmarks put in specifically to help people find their way. A large floor sculpture, a
wall mural, a fountain, an indoor garden could all serve people who are trying to remember directions. Walking down one
corridor after another can be confusing, even for "normals."

But if you can remember passing the wall mural, and turning at the fountain, finding your way becomes easier.

Indoor spaces should be designed with straight aisles. One drugstore chain has recently created angled aisles. When I am in the middle of one of those aisles I become completely disoriented. I have no idea which way to go to find the cashier or exit the store. The store may have been designed this way to encourage shopping by making sure people wander through more aisles and see more things. All it does for me and the other directionally challenged people I have spoken to is make us resolve to shop in other places.

Maps seem like a helpful device to put in the center of shopping malls, college campuses, and hospitals. For a person who has difficulty with mental rotation, however, a stationary map is nearly useless. It's possible to tell what floor a store is on by looking at a map like this, or what building is next to the one you want to find. However, if you can't pick up the map and turn it around to face the direction you are headed, it is not useful for much else. On the other hand, a three-dimensional map placed in a mall or on a school campus will provide usable information to the directionally challenged person.

Architects have long known that, when indoors, people can orient themselves more easily if they can see outside. Yet many large malls, hospitals, schools, parking structures, and office complexes have few windows; often the windows they have are not in helpful places, places where people might get disoriented, places where there is a choice of routes to take.

Why aren't all parking spaces numbered? If you knew you parked in space #56, even if you exited through a different door than you entered, you could find your car. Numbering parking spaces is a simple, cheap, and easy thing to do, and it would make a huge difference for those people who dread parking in large lots.

Road signs are often confusing. I shop at a mall off a highway 30 minutes from my house. When exiting the mall one sign says east to Detroit. The other sign says west to Lansing. I know Ann Arbor is west, yet to get home I have to follow the sign that says east to Detroit. Needless to say the first time I tried to get home from this mall I got hopelessly lost.

When my son was 16 he and I went to pick up my daughter from camp. My husband had written detailed directions to the camp and we had no trouble getting there. My son navigated and I drove. We switched roles on the way back. My son drove and I navigated. We were fine until we saw a sign to Ann Arbor. I told my son to follow the sign. He informed me that we wouldn't get home that way.

"It says Ann Arbor."

"It's the wrong way."

"Go that way."

"That won't take us home."

"We live in Ann Arbor. It says Ann Arbor. Go that way."

"No!"

"I'm your mother. Obey me."

We got lost.

Signs should be tested by the directionally challenged before they are permanently installed.

Some cars can now be equipped with a navigational device that will literally take you to your destination. These small car computers show you a map of your car on the road, and follow your car as it moves along. The computer talks to you as you go, telling you when to get on and off the highway, when to turn and the remaining distance to your destination. These devices are quite expensive, but the cost will probably decrease in the future. If you can afford one, it will give you a wonderful sense of freedom and the confidence to go any-place. If you rent a car in a strange city, get one with a navigational device. Hertz has them in their midsize and luxury cars for $6 a day. You'll be able to navigate unfamiliar expressways and streets with ease and comfort. Check with a car dealer for information on installing this navigational device for your vehicle. It runs about $2,000.

Finally, never tell people who are directionally challenged to sit up and pay attention and they'll get where they are going. That's like telling a person with chemical depression to get a grip on and stop complaining.

I have spent a great deal of my life lost. I know that scary feeling that comes when you walk out of a place and suddenly don't know where you are, that eerie almost dizzy feeling of total disorientation. I've felt the panic that rises up and envelops you when you can't recognize any street or building or landmark. Setting out alone on a strange road, in a new city, in a new country is never easy. But if you are directionally challenged like me, push yourself a little. Force down that fear. Accept and use the six senses you have. Look at the clear sky. Let the wind sweep your face and follow that path that curves and winds and turns. Go and enjoy. The more you do it, the easier it will become.

Afterword

Turn Left at the Porcupine

By Roger Rapoport

 very publisher dreams of receiving a manuscript he or she can't put down. After staying up half the night racing through the pages, it's a fast trip to the office and a phone call to deliver the good news to the author. Your book has been accepted; a contract is in the mail.

Although she didn't know it at the time, Linda Grekin's book was sold before the manuscript arrived on my desk at RDR Books. In fact, I had committed to it the minute I heard about it. Grekin, a Michigan school librarian, had been recommended to us by a bookstore in Oak Park, Michigan. The children's buyer, Colleen Kammer, suggested that Grekin's school would be an excellent place to stage an event for Randy, Tova, and Hanna Perrin, who had recently published a teen novel for RDR called *Time Like A River.*

The event was a huge success, and when it was over, Grekin asked Linda Cohen of our office if we'd be interested in seeing her manuscript on people who have a bad sense of direction. As a travel writer and publisher, I too have been lost all over the world. Surprisingly, in this age of information overload, I had never seen a good article on the subject, let alone a book. Unable to find any solid information on this problem that handicaps many millions, Grekin found an easy way to answer her own library research question. She wrote a book about it.

And what a book it is. Because there were no surveys available to her on the subject, Grekin designed her own with faculty help at the University of Michigan. Standing outside in bitter cold interviewing sample groups, canvassing students, reviewing the psychological literature on cognitive maps, Grekin has given us an important document that will hopefully stimulate further study on this fascinating problem.

The significance of this book is apparent to anyone who has ever gotten bad advice at a gas station or been told, as one magazine writer recalls, to "turn left at the porcupine." From the Donner Party that was given a "shortcut" through Utah that caused a tragic delay to Tom Wolfe's *Bonfire of the Vanities,* getting lost is an important part of American history and literature.

For the Donner group, being misrouted meant arriving late in the Sierras and being trapped in an early snowstorm. In Wolfe's novel, a master of the universe takes the wrong turn off the freeway and ends up in a tragic car accident in the Bronx. Both stories illustrate an important point. Any of us, not just the directionally impaired, can be given a bum steer. Even those who have good navigational skills can end up hopelessly lost. Consider, for example, the Northwest Airlines jet pilots flying to Frankfurt in 1995 when a Scottish air traffic controller gave them an erroneous heading for Brussels. Every passenger on the plane knew what was wrong because their route was projected on a movie screen. But the pilots, locked up front in the cockpit, had no access to that information and ended up landing in the wrong country.

Whether you are misdirected or simply can't find your way makes little difference. The consequences are identical. In her book, Grekin makes excellent suggestions on how to minimize this problem that can strike any of us. Drawing on travels at home and abroad, I would like to add a few of my own.

First, it is important to not assume that the map or the person giving you directions is always correct. I recently purchased a supposedly "new" map at a gas station near the Los Angeles airport only to find out, a couple of hours later, that major new highway construction was not showing on this very out-of-date piece of cartography. Second, don't assume the person giving you directions has ever been where you are going or really knows how to go there. Some years ago, Margot Lind and I were researching a series of maps for a cartographer. Fully three-quarters of the establishments we called could not tell us whether they were on the north, south, east, or west side of the street. Finally, and perhaps most important, don't assume that street numbers will work for you. I recently made a long drive down a major arterial in Pittsburgh and fully 70 percent of the buildings, including shopping centers, did not have street numbers. While this problem isn't as bad as in Japan, where buildings are not numbered sequentially, it is a critical issue.

Because a little humility goes a long way, try to approach navigation with a beginner's mind. Don't assume you know what you're doing. Recently, I was explaining the concept of Grekin's book to a college student in Kansas. "Right now," I said pointing straight ahead, "we're facing north. But a directionally impaired person would tell you that's south."

The young man looked at me quizzically and said, "I don't know how to tell you this, but actually, we're facing east."

About Linda Grekin

Linda Grekin is the librarian at the Hillel Day School in Farmington Hills, Michigan. Ms. Grekin graduated from the University of Michigan with degrees in journalism and education. She has taught school, developed educational curricula, worked as a free lance journalist, and jointly owned and operated Around Town Tours Inc., an Ann Arbor company that provides individual and group tours of the area.

Ms. Grekin lives in Ann Arbor with her husband, Roger, who is on the faculty of the University of Michigan Medical School. They have three grown children, Joe, Josh, and Emily. Locally, she has been lost in the Detroit Metropolitan Airport parking structure, the University of Michigan Graduate Library's 8th floor stacks, Briarwood Shopping Mall, and on I-275 between Detroit and Flint. Further afield, she has been lost repeatedly in woods, forests, and national parks.

Index

I Should Have
Stayed Home

The Worst Trips of Great Writers

One of "the five best travel books of the year. Feisty, funny, a bracing alternative to the Technicolor-sunset school of travel writing."
—San Francisco Examiner

Edited by
ROGER RAPOPORT *and*
MARGUERITA CASTANERA

In this national bestseller, 50 top travel writers, novelists, and journalists including **Isabel Allende, Jan Morris, Barbara Kingsolver, Paul Theroux, Mary Morris, Dominique Lapierre, Pico Iyer, Eric Hansen, Rick Steves, Tony Wheeler, and Mary Mackey** tell the stories of their greatest travel disasters. From the electric baths of Tokyo to the *Night of the Army Ants* in Guatemala, this unforgettable book will make you unfasten your seatbelt for the belly laugh of the travel season. Guaranteed to whet your appetite or make you cancel your reservations.

ISBN: 1-57143-014-8

$15.95
TRADE PAPERBACK
256 PAGES

I've Been Gone Far Too Long

Scientists' Worst Trips

Edited by MONIQUE BORGERHOFF-MULDER *and* WENDY LOGSDON

In this hilarious anthology, 26 research scientists go off the deep ends of the earth. Travel with a young researcher in Dian Fossey's camp as she is handed a gun and told to go out and shoot a gorilla poacher. See how a scientist reacts when he discovers a poisonous bushmaster in his bidet. From bush pilots and endangered species to Land Rover nightmares, this hair-raising book will keep you up past dawn. This book is a tribute to the courage of an intrepid band of researchers who have risked all to bring home the truth. Authors are contributing their royalties to the Wildlife Conservation Society.

ISBN: 1-57143-054-7

$15.95
TRADE PAPERBACK
296 PAGES

"People in khaki and pith helmets can be funny. Some could start second careers as comedians should they be denied tenure."
—American Library Association Booklist

After the Death of a Salesman

Business Trips to Hell

"*If you're interested in finding out just what it's like for the men and women of the road, this book offers a terrifically funny and occasionally touching insight*"

—American Library Association Booklist

By ROGER RAPOPORT

In this sequel to bestselling *I Should Have Stayed Home* and *I've Been Gone Far Too Long,* business people tell of their greatest travel disasters—from the emergency room to the paddy wagon. Read this book and you'll be happy you weren't traveling with: oilman Jack Howard, cruise scout Marcia Wick, engineer Joe Carr, conductor Murray Gross, bookseller Monica Holmes, investor Jack Branagh, sales rep Teri Goldsmith, or publisher Cynthia Frank. Dedicated to the memory of Willie Loman, this tribute to corporate road warriors includes an inside and affectionate look at the book publishing business and offers an amusing view of everything they don't want you to know in business school.

ISBN: 1-57143-062-8

$15.95
TRADE PAPERBACK
224 PAGES

Others Titles of Interest from RDR Books

WOMEN'S BOOKS

A Kind of Grace

Edited by Ron Rapoport

Ron Rapoport, popular commentator on National Public Radio's "Weekend Edition" and Deputy Sports Editor at the *Chicago Sun-Times,* brings together 66 wonderful stories on women athletes ranging from Billie Jean King and Martina Navratilova to the first woman to play high school football. Written by top sportswriters, this remarkable anthology is funny, heartbreaking, and beautifully written.

"Good Stuff.... Eloquent.... A powerful argument for gender equity ..."—Jim Murray, *Los Angeles Times*

ISBN 1-57143-013-X
$16.95 Paperback

Places of Greater Safety

By Hilda Hollingsworth

Hailed by critics on both sides of the Atlantic, this coming-of-age memoir tells the hidden story behind the largest evacuation of children ever staged. Hilda Hollingsworth's bittersweet tale shows the courage and ingenuity of young people forced to cope with fear and hardship.

Soon to be a major motion picture.

"Wonderfully written, evocative of its time, funny and sad ... written from the courage of the soul."

—Dirk Bogarde, *London Telegraph*

ISBN 0-9636161-1-0
$14.95 Paperback

The Virago Woman's Travel Guide to London

By Josie Barnard

London is lustrous, literary, and lewd. Josie Barnard captures all the many wonders of this famous city with a special emphasis on women's contributions to London's history, art, and culture.

ISBN 1-57143-017-2
$16.95 Paperback

Silvie's Life

By Marianne Rogoff

What do you do when doctors insist your new baby has only a short time to live? Marianne Rogoff answers this painful question in *Silvie's Life,* an autobiography of the heart that appeals to readers of all ages.

"*Silvie's Life* is a tender and beautifully written book. I stayed up all night reading it, absolutely mesmerized, in awe of Silvie's parents and of Silvie herself. I couldn't put it down."
—Anne Lamott

ISBN 1-57143-045-8
$9.95 Trade paperback

Time Pieces

By Rella Lossy

Time Pieces' three sections span four decades of Rella Lossy's life. A prize-winning UC Berkeley poet, Lossy published poetry widely—nationally and internationally. Her experiences with metastatic cancer inspired some powerful and sometimes humorous poems included in the section entitled Metronomes. She succumbed to that disease a week after sending *Time Pieces* to the printer.

"It is very fine poetry, unusual, and should be read."

—Anais Nin

ISBN 1-57143-060-1
$13.95 Trade paperback

Treasure

By Gina Davidson

One of the funniest books ever written about teenagers' parents. Gina Davidson's wry struggle to not be "the world's most hideous mother" of 13-going-on-21 Treasure, and her losing battle to "parent" will bring laughter to readers of all ages.

"A collection of droll essays on raising a teenager in London. Although she wrote some of its pieces for Britain's left-wing *Guardian,* her book is amusing enough to coax a smile out of Newt Gingrich."

—*Cleveland Plain Dealer*

ISBN 1-57143-023-7
$12.95 Paperback

HUMOR BOOKS

Wannabe Guide to Wine

By Jack Mingo

Do you want impress your friends and humiliate those you don't care for by mastering the art of wine snobbery? In this entertaining book, humorist Jack Mingo can instantly gratify your ambition! Now it's easy to sniff and swirl your way to the top.

ISBN 1-57143-039-3
$9.95 Trade paperback

Wannabe Guide to Golf

By Jack Mingo

It used to take years to sound like a golf pro. Not anymore. Funnyman Jack Mingo will teach you how to achieve your dream in the comfort of your easy chair ... with no green fees to pay! Mingo shows you how to look, act, and feel like a putter instead of a putz.

ISBN 1-57143-040-7
$9.95 Trade paperback

Wannabe Guide to Classical Music (March 1999)

By Bob Wieder

Do you think that the "Moonlight Sonata" was written by Sting? Swear Pachelbel is a Mexican fast food joint? Isn't it about time you stopped trying to fake it and face the music? Even if you can't tell a tenor from a basso profundo, this book will keep you in harmony. With the *Wannabe Guide to Classical Music* you'll never go off key when talking about Telemann.

ISBN 1-57143-055-5
$9.95 Trade paperback

BOOKS FOR CHILDREN

Time Like a River

By Randy Perrin with Tova and Hannah Perrin

This multicultural first novel written by Randy Perrin with his daughters, Tova, 14, and Hannah, 12, has been hailed by readers across America. This story of two families, one Jewish-American, the other Chinese-American, brought together in a miraculous journey across time and space has captivated readers of all ages.

"A truly amazing accomplishment. . . . The triumph of love over death and the willing of a miracle are important, engaging themes."

—Karen Cushman

American Library Association, Quick Picks Nominee

ISBN 1-57143-061-X
$14.95 Hardcover

The Best of Michael Rosen (Book and Tape)

By Michael Rosen
Illustrated by Quentin Blake
Introduction by Ken and Yetta Goodman

Wetlands Press is proud to offer this exciting poetry anthology by two of the most honored names in contemporary children's literature. Michael Rosen's bestselling titles, such as *We're Going on a Bear Hunt* and *How The Animal Got Their Colors,* have been hailed by critics around the world. Quentin Blake is famous for his award-winning illustrations that have accompanied the work of writers such as Roald Dahl.

"Michael Rosen is one of those rare people who have never lost touch with what it is like to be ten. He has the rare ability to convey childhood experience in language as simple and intense as the pleasures and pains it describes."

—*London Times*

ISBN 1-57143-046-6
$16.95 Hardcover

Also available on an unabridged 90 minute audio cassette, read by the author.

ISBN 1-57143-058-X
$11.95

Milton

By Ed Massey
Illustrated by Kristy Chu

Milton, wrapped up in "Cattle Hill," a painting, is off on the ultimate field trip, a story that travels beyond the walls of a museum excursion deep into the American heartland. Evocative of Grant Wood and Virginia Lee Burton, *Milton* is also fine art that celebrates a divine bovine.

Los Angeles sculptor Ed Massey has been praised for his imaginative work that highlights some of the key social and political issues of our day. New York artist Kristy Chu's dynamic paintings and murals have won acclaim from Manhattan to Taiwan. Both hold a Master's in Fine Arts from Columbia University.

ISBN 1-57143-074-4
$19.95 Hardcover

Dinosaur With An Attitude

By Hanna Johansen

Hilarious, mouthy, philosophical—that's compsognathus, the existential dinosaur with an attitude.

"A great deal of dino information is cleverly incorporated into the story."

—School Library Journal

ISBN 1-57143-018-0
$12.95 Hardcover

ISBN 1-57143-022-9
$7.95 Paperback

DARE TO LOVE US SERIES

Unloved creatures finally get equal time in this exciting new series. A kinesthetic design lets readers create animal figures by unfolding the pages. Sound chips teach kids how to recognize the distinctive sound of a snake's rattle or a wolf's howl.

The Wolf

By Roger Rapoport
Illustrated by Paul Kratter

Enter the magical realm of one of nature's most fascinating creatures. Learn how wolves help control the balance of nature, sing to one another, and use their tails to apologize.

ISBN 1-57143-049-0
$12.95 (Batteries Included)

The Rattler

By Roger Rapoport
Illustrated by Paul Kratter

Here's the book that tells you everything about rattlers: why they shake their tails 50 times per second, eat just once a week, smell with their tongues, and listen through their jawbones. Press the button to hear a real snake rattle.

ISBN 1-57143-050-4
$12.95 (Batteries Included)

THE GETAWAY GUIDES

Each of these guides is an ideal itinerary planner for short or long trips. Organized with daily trip schedules, each book gently guides you to well-known and off-the-beaten-track destinations with helpful directions, recommended schedules, and convenient lodging and dining recommendations. Written by experts who visit every one of the places they recommend, the Getaway Guides can be used for long weekends, week-long trips, or grand three week tours. Perfect for budget travelers and those who prefer luxury, each Getaway Guide is years in the making to insure that your trip is a winner from beginning to end. Selective and fun to read, each book reveals the secrets travel writers usually reserve for their closest friends.

The Getaway Guide to California

By Roger Rapoport

This up-to-the-minute guide showcases the best of the Golden State. The Pacific coast, the mountains, the wine country, San Francisco, Los Angeles, San Diego, Yosemite, Redwood country, the Monterey peninsula, Santa Barbara, and much more are easily seen thanks to convenient daily itineraries. The secrets travel writers keep to themselves are now yours. Fun to read and full of tips not found in any other guide.

ISBN 1-57143-068-7
$15.95
Available February 1999

The Getaway Guide to Agatha Christie's England

By Judith Hurdle

The world's second most widely read writer, Agatha Christie loved England. Now with the help of Judith Hurdle you can see why more than 2 billion readers have shared her fascination with towns like London, Wallingford, Harrogate, Torquay, and Burgh Island, as well as the Orient Express. In addition to showcasing Christie's many homes, you'll visit the town where she disappeared for 11 days and see the setting for many of her best-loved novels. A wonderful introduction to Britain, this literary companion also includes a close look at the author, her family, and her passion for archaeology. Even the most knowledgeable Christie reader will find this travel guide to Agatha's world hard to put down.

ISBN 1-57143-071-7
$15.95
Available January 1999

The Getaway Guide to the American Southwest

By Richard Harris

One of America's leading travel writers takes you on a grand tour of the Southwest from Mesa Verde to the Canyonlands and the Grand Canyon. From national parks to the best restaurants in Santa Fe, this guide to the very best of Southwestern Colorado, Utah, Arizona, and New Mexico includes big cities like Las Vegas and Phoenix as well as legendary Native American ruins. Organized with easy-to-follow daily itineraries, each trip is ideal for travelers of all ages.

ISBN 1-57143-073-3
$15.95
Available May 1999

The Getaway Guide to Colorado

By Roger Rapoport

The Colorado Rockies, long a favorite vacation destination, never looked better. This book takes you from mile-high Denver out to Steamboat Springs and Glenwood Canyon, Aspen, Vail, and Telluride. Each day's itinerary is carefully organized to insure the very best sightseeing, hotels, and restaurants. Written for budget travelers and those who can afford to go first class, this book highlights the best historic train rides, hot springs, ski resorts, ghost towns, and urban delights.

ISBN 1-57143-072-5
$15.95
Available June 1999

Our books are available at your local bookstore. For more information or a free catalog contact RDR Books at 4456 Piedmont Avenue, Oakland, CA 94611. Phone (510) 595-0595. Fax (510) 595-0598. Email: rdrbooks@lanminds.com.

See our books on the Web at http: //users.lanminds.com/~rdr-books.